Ziryab

AUTHENTIC
ARAB CUISINE

Ziryab

AUTHENTIC ARAB CUISINE

Table Conversations,
Travel Notes, and Recipes—
A Practical Introduction to Arab Gastronomy

Farouk Mardam-Bey
Illustrations by Odile Alliet

ici
la
PRESS

English translation rights © 2002 by Ici La Press

Copyright © 1998 ACTES SUD

Illustrations: Odile Alliet
Cover Illustration: Hadîth Bayâd wa Riyâd

Published by Ici La Press
694 Main St. South
Woodbury, CT 06798
www.icilapress.com

Printed in Singapore by Imago

ISBN 1-931605-02-5

10   9   8   7   6   5   4   3   2   1

For Soulayma

TABLE OF CONTENTS

Foreword

Abu al-Hasan 'Ali ibn Nafi' was born in Iraq in 789 C.E. His family, however, most likely originated in Persia. With a melodious voice, dark skin, and gentle manners, he was nicknamed Ziryab, the name of the harmoniously mellow black bird. He received a solid education in the humanities and sciences, especially in geography and astronomy, and eventually became the favorite disciple of Ishaq al-Mawsili, the Abbasid court's most famous musician and singer. Nevertheless, resentment replaced the preferential treatment he received by his master Ishaq al-Mawsili who became envious of Ziryab's immense success with the great caliph Harun al Rashid to whom he had introduced his protégé. As a result, Ziryab had to leave his country when he was just thirty years old.

So Ziryab traveled west to pursue his fame and fortune, and after a short stay in Tunisia, he eventually settled in Cordoba in 822 C.E. His arrival in Spain could not have been more perfectly timed as the emir 'Abd al-Rahman had recently lost his father, and the new Umayyiad caliph wished to compete with the Baghdadi sultans in extravagance and refinement. Subsequently, the immigrant was received with the highest regards. He was awarded a very generous pension, along with frequent special bonuses and the rent of several houses and orchards. His musical talent, his encyclopedic knowledge and the utmost distinction of his manners soon captivated the prince, and charmed the whole of Muslim Spain.

Ziryab was an innovator in music. Despite the fact that he was a Middle Easterner himself, he founded what was then known as the Andalusian School of Music. He invented the five-string lute and imposed the use of eagle claw plectrums. Above all, he was an advocate for a new art of living, the successor of Petronius and the predecessor of Brummel as told by Evariste Lévi-Provençal,[1] one of the most illustrious historians of Spanish Islam.

Ziryab first taught the people of Cordoba the most elaborate recipes of Baghdad's cuisine, as well as the sequence of plates for an elegant meal. It was no longer acceptable to serve the dishes together; they had to start with soups, then meat, followed by exquisitely spiced fowl dishes, and finish with sweets, walnuts, almonds and honey cakes, or vanilla-flavored preserved fruits filled with pistachios and hazelnuts. He wanted the aroma of the food to send the saliva under the tongue, and the sight of the table to bring pleasure to the eye. As for tablecloths, he did away with coarse linens and replaced them with fine leather; he proved that precious crystal stem-glasses suited the table setting better than gold or silver goblets. His innovations in the esthetics of living culminated in the opening of an institute of beauty in Cordoba, where people could learn the art of make-up, how to wax their body-hair, how to use tooth paste, and even how to style their hair. He instructed individuals to have their hair cut short and round, uncovering their eyebrows, the napes of their necks, and their ears, instead of keeping their hair long and allowing their parted hair to fall sloppily over their foreheads and temples. He established a fashion calendar which decreed that people should dress in white from early June through late September, and that spring would be the season for light silk gowns and bright colored tunics, and winter the time for quilted cloaks and fur coats. People sought his advice, and followed it word for word. The influence of the delicate and elegant 'Abbasid culture could not have been more direct, or more profound. Under

---

[1] *Histoire de l'Espagne musulmane*, 3 vol., Maisonneuve, Paris, Brill, Leyde, 1950–1967

Ziryab's unchallenged leadership, both courtiers and city-dwellers transformed the way individuals dressed, furnished their houses, and cooked their meals. Even many centuries later, the Arabic Petronius' name could be heard every time a new fashion appeared in the salons of the Spanish peninsula.

Knowing all that, I must have been very presumptuous, for six years, to have signed my modest culinary chronicles with the pseudonym Ziryab. Now that I am taking the risk of compiling them into one book, I would like to thank *Qantara*, the magazine of the *Institut du Monde Arabe* where they were published for the first time, and all my readers for not holding this against me.

I

Praise

Ziryab celebrates fourteen fruits and vegetables in addition to couscous, rice and cracked wheat, illustrating his often humorous words and his time-honored recipes.

The eggplant

THE RICH AND FAMOUS have often ridiculed the eggplant, out of sheer snobbery at first, or so it seems to me, because the beautiful black berry has always been a favorite of the poor. There is this anecdote which can be found in many a classic work: To a commoner who was praising the eggplant, especially when it is stuffed with meat, a scholar once replied, he would not have it, even stuffed with mercy! Still, it would be fair to see in this behavior the pernicious influence of certain physicians. The great Islamic physician Razes himself, in his *Book of Food Correctives*, claimed that "the eggplant is useless for the head." He was a man of good taste and he did acknowledge a few virtues to the eggplant, including the fact that even the weakest stomach easily digests it, but he was quick to add that an excessive consumption of the vegetable results in conjunctivitis and atrabilious diseases. And this was nothing in comparison with the allegations of his more blunt disciples, who went as far as to claim that the eggplant led to melancholy and madness.

Thus, the next step, for many people, was to consider the eggplant itself to be an evil vegetable. They explained that the word *badhinjan*—the eggplant in Arabic—came from *bad al-jan*, i.e. "the djinn (the devil) has laid eggs"! The evil reputation of the eggplant swept the Mediterranean, and it consequently was prohibited in England in the 16th century C.E. In Turkey it was also blamed for being the cause of the five hundred fires that devastated Istanbul during the Ottoman era. It is said that during eggplant season, in the height of summer, all the city dwellers would use live charcoal on their doorsteps in order to grill their favorite vegetable, without paying any heed to the wind that was then

3

sweeping through their city. This wind is still called *patlican metemi*, "the eggplant wind"!

This is to say that bad luck has always clung to the eggplant. But, in spite of that reputation it had remained, for the poor, the princess of all vegetables. As far as I am concerned, I don't know of any other vegetable that is as adaptable as the eggplant. You can eat it grilled or fried, boiled or braised, as a starter or an entree, with salt or with sugar. This probably explains why they say in Alep, Syria, of somebody who is always available to help others, or possibly is a perfectionist, that one "is like the eggplant."

The Arab cooks, in the classical age, were not wrong in reserving for our vegetable a place of honor in their treatises as did Baghdadi, for instance, or his anonymous counterpart in the Almuhad empire, or Ibn Razin—also a Maghrebi,[1] who lived at the time of the Merinids. Many more cooks, Muslims, Jews or Christians, in the Mediterranean countries, joined in the praise. I dare to state that nowhere else was the eggplant better treated than in the Arab countries, even though the Turks have excellent reasons to justify their claim of superior usage. Just look at the beaming street merchants in Damascus and listen to them melodiously praise its color, "darker than night," its volume, "just big enough for the pan," and its fleshy pulp "that will fry in water."

To accommodate such a marvel, the number of recipes is obviously innumerable. In Maghreb, Morocco's fried eggplant *tadgine* seems unequaled to me with a shoulder of lamb, veal knuckles, or a chicken. If you want to cook it, be sure to sprinkle it with salt, let it rest for an hour, and drain the water out before frying the eggplant. This is a basic principle by which one must abide every time one wishes to fry the eggplant. And do not forget saffron and ginger in your *tadgine*. I would also suggest Algeria's *mderbel*, a delicious stew with fried eggplants, lamb and chickpeas, flavored with black pepper, cinnamon and caraway

[1]Western Northern Africa, i.e., Morocco, Algeria, Tunisia

4

seeds. Sometimes it is even better to add chopped basil to it. They make the same dish in Tunisia, but then they also put seeded, peeled tomatoes and fresh hot pepper in it. It is delicious, too, provided you do not ruin it with *harissa*.[2]

If you asked me now to select from among the Eastern recipes, I would have to admit my embarrassment at being incapable of choosing. The eggplant's home, so to speak, is the Near East. However, if I really had to name a prize-winning recipe, I would first nominate *makdus*, because you can eat it first thing in the morning, for breakfast. This unequaled pickle is made with small eggplants that are slit lengthwise along one side, filled with walnuts, garlic, sprinkled with salt, and then preserved in olive oil. For a starter, I would add *baba ghannouj*, a large eggplant grilled in its skin, preferably over charcoal, then peeled, pounded and mixed with garlic, crushed with salt and a little pomegranate juice for acidity. Prepared this way, this very popular dish is a real treat for the palate, as well as the eye, if, before sprinkling it with olive oil, you decorate it with walnuts and pomegranate seeds. Another starter is *mutabbal*, fried crushed eggplants mixed with salted yogurt and garlic, *tahini* (sesame paste) and very finely minced parsley. Of course, I cannot fail to mention the famous *imam bayildi*—called the "fainting imam" because an erudite imam is said to have fainted from pleasure when he ate it the first time. The *imam bayildi* is prepared with small eggplants slit lengthwise along one side and filled with a mixture of pre-cooked tomatoes, onions cut in half moons, garlic and salt. First, arrange the pieces in a pan, then pour in water and some olive oil, keep them cooking over a hot fire, and let them simmer for half an hour. From among the main dishes, I would definitely mention *mussaqqa'a*, which is famous in France, though we do not use white sauce or grated cheese. Then I would mention two or three kinds of stews, and finally *maqluba*, which is very popular among the Palestinians, an elaborate esthetic arrangement of rice, eggplant and

[2]Tunisia's hot pepper paste

knuckle-joint of lamb, flavored with *quatre épices* (pepper, nutmeg, cinnamon and cloves), decorated with ground meat, almonds, and pine nuts. There are also many recipes where the eggplants are filled with rice or rice and meat, or with meat and pine nuts. Along with the *kebbes*, they are definitely considered the most delicious dishes in Near Eastern cuisine.

I do not wish to conclude without mentioning a few words on the stunning eggplant jam for dessert or breakfast. To make it, you need the very small and tender berries that are not easy to get in the marketplace. If you do manage to purchase some, do not forget that they must first be parboiled, and then each one pricked with a clove before being dipped in sugar syrup.

Admit that a djinn capable of giving us such beautiful eggs cannot be so evil.

Eggplant Ratatouille

Za'luka

ALGERIA

Serves 4

2 lbs. eggplants
4 garlic cloves
1 dry hot pepper
1 tsp. paprika
1 tsp. cinnamon
1 tsp. ground caraway
¾ cup olive oil
1 tbsp. vinegar
Salt

Peel and dice the eggplants, blanch them in boiling water, then drain and place in a pot.

Soak the dried pepper in hot water to soften. With a mortar and pestle, grind together the garlic, hot pepper, paprika, cinnamon, caraway, and a little salt. Add half a cup of water and mix it in.

Pour this *dersa* (spice paste) and the olive oil over the eggplants, mix and cook for 10 minutes over medium heat, simmer for 20 minutes. When the eggplants are cooked, add the vinegar.

Serve cold, as a starter.

Eggplant Purée

Baba ghannouj
SYRIA

Serves 4

2 large round eggplants
4 to 6 tbsp. tahini *(sesame paste)*
2 cloves garlic
2 to 3 tbsp. pomegranate juice
2 tbsp. cracked walnuts
1 pomegranate (optional)
Parsley
Salt
Olive oil

Char the eggplants over a flame or put them under the broiler, then peel them while still hot under a thin stream of cold water. Crush the garlic with a little salt.

Mash the eggplants with a wooden pestle or a fork. Mix the paste with the garlic, *tahini*, and the pomegranate juice.

Arrange the eggplant purée in a serving dish, top with the walnuts, minced parsley, and pomegranate seeds, then sprinkle with olive oil.

Chicken with Fried Eggplant

Djeb b-dbenjal

MOROCCO

Serves 6

1 large free-range chicken cut in 8 pieces
4½ lbs. eggplants
1 clove garlic
1 tsp. ginger
½ tsp. saffron powder
1½ cups oil
¾ cup lemon juice
1 tsp. flour
Salt

Cut off the stems of the eggplants and reserve, slice the eggplants in two across, and set them aside in salted water. Half peel the eggplants by leaving regular strips of the purple skin on the vegetable, then cut in thick rounds, salt lightly and allow to sweat off excess water for half an hour.

Pat the eggplants dry and fry them. Set aside on paper towels. Simmer the chicken with the crushed garlic, ginger, saffron, oil, two pinches of salt and a cup of water over medium heat, covered with a lid. Add water if necessary while the chicken is cooking.

Take the chicken out of the pot and drop the eggplant stems into the sauce. When they are cooked, add half of the lemon juice, bring the mixture to a boil, then put the chicken back into the pot.

Reheat the eggplant rounds in a frying pan, mash them with a fork, and pour out the surplus oil.

When ready to serve, reheat the mashed eggplant and stir in the rest of the lemon juice. Also reheat the chicken pieces and place them on a serving dish surrounded by the eggplant stems. Thicken the sauce with a little flour mixed with water; pour the sauce over the chicken mixture. Spoon the mashed eggplants on top.

Stuffed Eggplants with Olive Oil
Yalangi badhinjan
SYRIA

Serves 6

2 lbs. small eggplants
2 cups rice
1 cup finely minced onions
⅔ cup olive oil
1½ cups tomato juice
½ cup pine nuts
A handful of raisins
1 tsp. cinnamon
Salt
Pepper

Sauté the onions in the olive oil until lightly colored. Add the rice and cook until golden brown, then add the tomato juice with a little water. Simmer until all the liquid is absorbed. Cool. Add the salt, pepper, cinnamon, raisins, and pine nuts. Mix.

Cut off, wash, and peel the eggplant stems. Scoop out the pulp with a spoon and then wash the eggplants. Stuff them with the rice, mixture two thirds full, and top them with their stems. Arrange the eggplants next to each other in a pot, cover them with boiling water and simmer over low heat for 45 minutes. Serve cold.

Stuffed Eggplants with Pita Bread

Fattet al-makdus

SYRIA

Serves 6

2 lbs. small eggplants
¾ lb. ground lamb shoulder
3 onions
¾ cup yogurt
2 cloves garlic, crushed with a little salt
2 tbsp. tahini *(sesame paste)*
2 tbsp. tomato paste
2 tbsp. pomegranate concentrate
Parsley
2 grilled pita breads
½ cup pine nuts
Samn *(mix of butter and olive oil) or butter*
Salt and pepper

After removing the stems scoop the pulp out of the unpeeled eggplants and stuff them with the fried ground meat. Sauté the stuffed eggplants lightly in the *samn* or butter.

Cut the onions in half moon slices and sauté them in a pot until golden color. Add four cups of water and the tomato paste. Salt the mixture and simmer for 15 minutes.

Add pomegranate concentrate to the pot, then add the stuffed eggplants. Simmer for 15 minutes.

Mix the yogurt with the garlic and *tahini.*

Place the cut-up pita pieces in the bottom of a soup tureen, and pour some of the liquid from the pot on the pitas. Next pour in the yogurt and place the eggplants on top. Sprinkle with the rest of the fried ground meat and a little minced parsley.

Brown the pine nuts in *samn* and sprinkle them on top.

Eggplants Stuffed with Meat

Badhinjan mahchi

LEBANON

Serves 4

2 lbs. small eggplants
3 cups tomato juice
2 cloves crushed garlic
1 lb. ground lamb shoulder
½ cup pine nuts
3 tbsp. samn *(mix of butter and olive oil)*
Salt, pepper

Brown the pine nuts. Lightly sauté the meat, sprinkle with salt and pepper, and mix in the pine nuts.

Peel the eggplants and fry them half way before slitting them open lengthwise with a knife. Remove the seeds. Stuff the eggplant with the meat and pine nut mixture and arrange them in a baking dish.

Add the tomato juice and garlic, then put them in the oven. Bake at 350°F for 30 minutes.

Serve hot with rice or angel hair pasta.

Eggplants with Rice
Maqluba
PALESTINE

Serves 6

4½ lbs. eggplants
1½ lbs. deboned lamb shoulder, cut in pieces
½ lb. ground lamb shoulder
2½ cups Basmati rice
2 onions
½ cup pine nuts
½ cup slivered almonds
Samn (mix of butter and olive oil)
Oil for frying
Salt and pepper
Nutmeg, cinnamon, cloves

Wash the rice carefully and soak it for one hour in warm water. Peel the eggplants, cut them in medium-sized rounds, salt lightly and allow to sweat off excess water for half an hour. Cook the pieces of meat in water, skimming several times, add salt and pepper. Fry the eggplants and set them aside on paper towels. Cut the onions in half-moon slices, and brown them.

In a pot, layer first the onions and half of the meat, then half of the eggplants, then half of the rice. Repeat with the rest of the ingredients in the same order, sprinkle the top layer of rice with a pinch of salt and the spices. Slowly pour over the meat broth, just barely covering the layered mixture. Cover and simmer over medium heat for 10 minutes and reduce to very low heat until all the broth is absorbed. Remove the pot from the fire and let rest for 5 minutes. During this time, lightly sauté the ground meat with the almonds and pine nuts.

Turn the *maqluba* mixture into a big circular serving dish and top with the meat-almond-pine nut mixture.

Serve with yogurt seasoned with some crushed garlic.

The fava bean

To PRAISE IT, people call it "the poor man's meat." But if we stress its enormous nutritive value, we should raise it to an unrivaled social status. Actually, the origins and history of the fava bean is universal. It is loaded with mysteries, much more than with proteins and mineral salts. It may even contain the most profound of all secrets, the secret of life and death. Undoubtedly, in Egypt, the fava's birthplace four thousand years ago, the priests of Egypt believed in its mystical power and called the "fava field," the place where the souls of the departed were to wait before reincarnation. Orpheus and Pythagoras in Greece believed it too, so much so that their disciples were forbidden to eat it. It is said that one day a group of enemies were running after Pythagoras, and he chose to surrender and be killed, rather than walk across a field of fava beans, which would have interrupted the cycle of his reincarnation.

Commonly, the fava bean at that time was symbolized by the embryo, the first fruits of the earth—it held the future. People offered the fava to the Invisible World at the inauguration of spring rites. During wedding ceremonies, each bean represented the male child the couple was looking forward to. Even today, the fava, which is concealed in the French *Galette des Rois*, perpetuates that tradition. The person who finds it on the day of the Epiphany is called the king of the day, and the others must pay homage to him. Speaking of the embryo, the fava bean is often replaced by a tiny baby doll. It was once china, but now it is plastic!

This symbolism is unknown in classic Arab literature, except maybe for a few esoteric writers. But, the old pythagorian interdiction, justified for medical reasons, does not seem fortuitous.

As early as in the 2nd century of Hegira, Ibn Qutayba, on the assertions of a Greek physician, claimed that eating fava beans weakens the eyesight and triggers dreams that are so befuddled that nobody can interpret them. A century later, the Andalusian Ibn ʿAbd Rabbih blamed the fava for causing "ill dispositions." Later, the great master of Cordoba, Averroes, joined in, and suggested that the fava might "deteriorate our thought processes." About the same time, in the Orient, Ibn al-Jawzi, a strict Hanbali law-specialist, accused it of a more trivial consequence: creating gas in the stomach of those who eat it.

As always, only the poets were wise enough to see the truth. Certainly, they were not interested in the dry bean, which doesn't lend itself easily to the delights of rhetoric, but their lines about the plant in bloom could fill a whole *diwan*.[1] The beautiful fava flowers—white, purple, and dotted with one black spot inside each of their wings—were bound to evoke butterflies, gazelle eyes, spotted white doves, and even a silver jewel with one black pearl. I'd rather leave you to imagine the very many risqué metaphors of the later poets, those geniuses of futility, as they contemplated the velvety horn-shaped green pods, or the fresh beans on their delicate, smooth, soft skin.

Still, from the culinary treatises that have survived the times, it seems that the fava did not inspire the cooks of the Golden Age. Baghdadi, for instance, only cites two or three rather banal recipes. The fava did not fare any better with the Andalusians. Their rare recipes are a far cry from those of their Moroccan successors. I am thinking of the exquisite *tadjine* with fresh fava and artichoke bottoms. I truly believe that the combination of these two vegetables—with or without meat—is still the most refined way of cooking the fresh fava. It is common in most Arab countries, as well as in Turkey, where they cook fava as a great starter

[1] A council presided over by a sultan

16

with dill. In Algeria—a country whose cuisine is unfairly under-estimated—they have at least ten recipes that would be worth presenting here. This is not possible, but I want to cite two fava recipes with *dersa*, a mixture of garlic, black and red pepper, hot pepper and salt, to which you add some olive oil and a handful of finely minced fresh cilantro, and couscous with fava beans. The beans are first steamed, and then added to a lamb shoulder broth with saffron and two kinds of pepper. In these recipes, the fava must cook in its pod; the tips are cut off and the pod is cut in two or three pieces. In Syria and Lebanon, they often use the whole pod to cook *ful muqalla* (fava fried in olive oil), which you can find on every table in Damascus during the fava season. They are also crazy about *fuliyyah* (a fava stew) that is cooked with a mutton knuckle, some garlic and fresh cilantro, and *ruzz bil-ful* (fava with rice) when the fresh beans are cooked together with a lamb joint. This combination of lamb and fresh beans ennobles the two ingredients to the rank of pistachios. Finally, there is another Syrian-Lebanese recipe, which you can read below. I believe it is even better as it uses yogurt with the fava.

Now, I would like to discuss the dried fava beans. First, there are the larger ones, which you soak overnight in cold water, drain, soak once more, drain again, and then boil. They can be eaten as a salad, or better still, just the way they are, peeled and sprinkled with salt and ground cumin. And then there are the smaller ones, which are used to make the famous *ful midammis* all over the Middle East. It is especially popular in Egypt, where there are one thousand and one ways to cook it. If you want to cook it right, do not cook the beans in a pressure cooker, and do not add any salt, as it is sometimes suggested in a few cookbooks. If you do, the only thing you will get is ugly black beans floating in an ugly swill. Actually, the surest method is to add a tablespoon of coral lentils and another tablespoon of round rice, and then let the fava beans simmer overnight at low heat. The *ful* is even better if it is cooked, as it once was, in a big earthenware pot on the coolest corner of an old fashioned stove.

There is, finally, the number one dish, *ta'miyya*, or falafel. In Egypt, they make the paste by mixing the broken fava beans with chives, parsley, garlic, dill, cilantro, ground coriander, cumin, hot pepper and, optionally, fresh mint. In Syria, Lebanon and Palestine, they add chickpeas, but do without all the greens, except for the parsley. They make small balls, which are rolled in sesame seeds and then fried until golden in oil. Falafel is good, it is filling, it is healthy, and it is as good as all the fast-food hamburgers in the world!

Dry Fava Bean Soup

Bissara

EGYPT

Serves 6

3 cups large dry fava beans (shelled)
3 tsp. dried mint
1 tsp dry koret* powder (optional)
3 onions
1 garlic clove
2 lemons
Olive oil
2 grilled pita breads, cut into bite-sized pieces
5 cups water

Soak the beans in water for 24 hours. Drain and cook them in 5 cups of water over low heat, in a stainless steel or heavy-bottomed pot.

Cut the onions in thin half-moon slices and sauté them in a little oil until golden brown. Add the minced garlic and sauté another minute.

Once the beans are cooked, purée them and mix them with the pepper, mint, and koret. Bring the mixture to a boil, stirring constantly.

Serve the *bissara* in individual bowls and top with *tadliya* (a garlic and onion mixture). Serve the grilled pita pieces and lemon slices separately.

*Koret (*molokheya*) is one of the bitter herbs in a Jewish Seder.

Fava Beans with Sesame Cream

Ful midammis bil-tihina

EGYPT

Serves 4

1¼ cups dry fava beans
1 tbsp. orange lentils
1 tbsp. round rice
½ cup tahini (sesame paste)
Juice of 2 lemons
1 tsp. salt
½ tsp. cayenne pepper
½ cup parsley

Soak the beans for 3 hours in lukewarm water then drain.

Put the beans in a heavy pot, cover with boiling water, add the lentils and the rice, and let them simmer overnight over very low heat.

Just before serving, reheat the beans and prepare the sauce by mixing the *tahini* with a little water, the lemon juice, and the garlic (which has been crushed with salt and cayenne pepper).

Pour the *tahini* sauce into a deep serving dish, top with the hot fava beans, and then sprinkle with very finely chopped parsley.

Fava Beans in a Sauce

Ros bratel

ALGERIA

Serves 6

2 lbs. very fresh green fava beans in the pods
6 tbsp. olive oil
1 cup chopped cilantro
4 garlic cloves
1 tsp. paprika
1 tsp. cayenne pepper
Salt and pepper
1 tbsp. flour
1 tbsp. vinegar

Snip off the ends of the bean pods and rinse them well. Cut the pods into 1 inch pieces and place them flat in a heavy-bottomed pot.

Add the garlic, which has been crushed with salt, along with the cilantro, spices and the oil. Sauté the mixture about 5 minutes before adding 1½ cups of water. Simmer the mixture over low heat until the beans are tender.

Mix the flour with the vinegar and a little of the juice from the beans, pour into the fava beans and stir slowly while simmering a few more minutes.

Serve cold as a starter.

Green Fava Bean Stew

Marquit ful

TUNISIA

Serves 4

1¼ lbs. deboned lamb shoulder
1¼ lbs. fresh green fava beans, in the pods
½ lb. spinach
2 onions
¼ cup dry white beans (soaked overnight and drained)
¾ cup olive oil
1 tbsp. tomato paste
½ cup parsley
1 tsp. paprika
Salt and pepper

Cut the meat in large cubes and season with salt and pepper. Sauté with chopped onions. Dilute the tomato paste in a little water, add with the white beans and paprika. Cover with water and cook an hour over low heat.

Meanwhile, chop the spinach and parsley and cut the fava bean pods into one-inch pieces. Add these vegetables to the meat mixture and simmer 30 more minutes, covered.

Fava Beans with Yogurt

Fuliyyah bil-laban

SYRIA and LEBANON

Serves 6

2 lbs. shelled fava beans
1¼ lbs. lamb shanks, cut in large cubes
8 cups yogurt
1 onion, finely chopped
3 garlic cloves, crushed with salt
1 tbsp. butter
2 tbsp. cornstarch
A few drops of vinegar
1 egg

Sauté the meat and onion with half of the garlic.

Add the fava beans, cover the mixture and cook for a few minutes. Pour in two cups of boiling water and simmer 45 minutes over low heat.

Meanwhile, beat the egg, add in the remaining garlic and the vinegar. Mix the cornstarch in a little cold water. Stir the cornstarch and the egg into the yogurt.

Put this yogurt mixture over the heat and bring to a boil, stirring constantly with a wooden spoon.

Pour the yogurt into the fava stew and place the stew back on the heat to cook for a few minutes.

Serve immediately with rice.

Green Fava Bean Dessert

Mhallabiyyah bil-ful

SYRIA

Serves 6

8 cups milk
1 cup sugar
2 tbsp. cornstarch
½ cup cream of rice
1¼ lbs. very tender green fava beans in the pods
2 tbsp. orange flower water

Scald the milk. Add the sugar and cream of rice (which has been mixed in one cup of cold water). Bring to a boil a second time, and then simmer for 30 minutes.

Shell and peel the outer layer of the fava beans, add to the milk mixture, and cook another 10 minutes.

Make a paste by diluting cornstarch in little water. Add this paste to the fava bean mixture and simmer a few minutes to thicken, stir with a wooden spoon.

Remove the pan from the heat. Add the orange flower water and pour into individual bowls.

Serve chilled.

Saffron

SAFFRON IS THE result of a double wound. According to the Greeks, Hermes accidentally wounded his friend Crocos while throwing his discus. Crocos died at once, but Hermes willed that his friend's blood droplets, which were sprinkled about on the ground, turn into strange small flowers, each with three stamens. The strong aroma and bright color of Crocos' flowers were to make saffron, the most precious of all spices.

The same legend relates that Hermes also metamorphosed the nymph Smilax, who was passionately in love with Crocos, into a saffron flower. The two lovers were to be united forever in the heart of the flower. Maybe the most celebrated characteristic of saffron at that time originated from the ultimate victory of love over death. It was believed to be an aphrodisiac. This is probably why Homer said that Zeus himself used and abused it; he went so far as to fill up his bed with saffron pistils. Accordingly, the wealthy Romans took up the idea and would sprinkle saffron on the sheets of young married couples. The Satiricon claims that they used it extravagantly in their banquets, but it was probably more to show off their wealth than to enhance their urge for love.

Saffron does not only have the color of gold, it has, so to speak, the same value as gold. The stamens must be picked by hand, and the harvesting has been done in the same way for thousands of years, as evidenced in a fresco you can still see in the palace in Knossos, Crete. You need no less than one hundred fifty thousand flowers to get one kilo of the spice.[1] This is why the old Greeks (and the Egyptians with their famous *kuphi* drug) tended

---

[1] That is, 68,000 flowers for one pound.

to use this aromatic spice for medicinal purposes, or dye special pieces of cloth for ritual purposes, as in Tyre, where newly-wed women used to wear a saffroned veil to show that they had finally achieved all attributes of their femininity. In medieval Europe, once the Arabs introduced it in Spain between the 8th and 10th centuries C.E., saffron was to serve the same purpose. It was used as a medicine and to dye cloth. For instance, the most famous physicians in Salerno praised its power to make people laugh, while the cloth merchants from Tuscany in Italy, up to the Hanseatic cities of Germany, used it to dye their fabrics. It is said that saffron sometimes served as collateral for financial operations in Florence, where it was especially popular.

In classical Islam, as elsewhere, saffron obviously preoccupied the physicians. Some, Razes among them, did not want to have anything to do with it, because it was rumored to induce nausea and insomnia, while others, like Avicenna, favored it for its effects on the "substance of the vital spirit." However, it is certain that it was successfully used as a salve to reduce scar tissue, soothe gout and heal cataracts. Cultivated in small quantities in the Arab Near East, and in larger quantities in Iran and Turkey, saffron then swept over Maghreb, from where it was introduced into Spain, which became its place of predilection. Sevilla's agronomist Ibn al-'Awwaam described it in great detail in the late 12th century C.E. On quite another plane, the saffron flower with its three stamens also attracted a crowd of poets and landscape artists of the post-classical period. In the saffron flower, they saw "flamboyant sulphur threads," "shy maidens," or sometimes "three damsels embracing." And the number of references to its gold-yellow color or its gold value is innumerable.

Still, saffron has always been especially appreciated for its strong fragrance. The King in the Song of Solomon mentions it in order to evoke the smell of the beloved woman. More prosaically, we know that it was used throughout the centuries in all countries around the Mediterranean Sea to season dishes. There is a 14th century French cookbook with over 70 out of 172 recipes using saffron (or safflower for color). Only a few recipes are still known, but they are generally the most famous of France's regional dishes, such as *bouillabaisse* in Marseille, or *mourtayrol*, a saffron soup from the South West. And saffron is also found in many a liqueur recipe, among them the famous elixir of the monks of the Carthusian order. As for the Italians, they have been crazy about Siena's saffron *panforte* since the Middle Ages. Spain produces the best saffron in the world and obviously uses it frequently. Only the Spanish *paella* is well-known abroad, and not always cooked right at that!

No country in the world knows and honors saffron as much as Morocco. Of course, the Arabs in the Near East know about it. They sprinkle their rice dishes or desserts with it, for instance *balouza*, which is a variation of the classical *faloudhaj*. The inhabitants of Alep mix it with musk for their *zarda*, a rice cake they offer at wedding ceremonies. Nevertheless, nowhere is saffron more revered than in Moroccan cuisine. It is used in abundance in Morocco, and to a lesser extent in Algeria and Tunisia. You can find it in a variety of ethnic dishes, like *couscous, harina, chorba, bastella*, and also a great number of *tadjines* (following are two very simple recipes). The Tunisians and the Algerians also use saffron in their stews and roasts. Finally, the Moroccans add saffron to their *griouch*, a delicious doughnut drenched in honey and sprinkled with sesame seeds.

Do I need to be very clear? Saffron has nothing to do with vulgar safflower, also known as "bastard saffron." Safflower adds color but does not offer taste, and it is produced in large quantities. This is why a few dishonest merchants have frequently been tempted to sell it as saffron. But, I would strongly advise people against the practice: a German spice merchant, who tried it, was burnt at the stake in 1344 at the marketplace, along with his second-rate goods!

White Beans with Saffron

Lubia b-za'faran

MOROCCO

Serves 6

1 lb. dried white beans
3 onions
1 tsp. pepper
½ tsp. crushed saffron threads
7 tbsp. samn (mix of butter and olive oil) or butter
½ cup parsley
Salt

Soak the beans overnight. Drain. Put them in a heavy pot with one finely chopped onion. Add the *samn* or butter, season with salt, pepper, and saffron, cover with water, bring to a boil. Cook over medium heat for 50 minutes, add more water if necessary.

Chop the parsley and add it to the beans with the remaining two onions, sliced in thin rounds.

After 10 to 15 minutes remove from the heat.

Sweet Potato Salad

Btata hlua b-za'faran

MOROCCO

Serves 4

2 lbs. sweet potatoes
1 tsp. pepper
½ tsp. crushed saffron threads
1 tsp. crushed cinnamon stick
¼ cup vegetable oil
2 tbsp. samn *(mix of butter and olive oil) or butter*
2 tbsp. sugar
Salt

Peel and dice the sweet potatoes. In a pot cook them covered with two cups of water, the oil, *samn* or butter, the spices, 1 tsp. of salt and the sugar.

When the potatoes are cooked, remove from the pot and reduce the sauce.

Serve hot or cold.

Lamb Tadgine with Potatoes

Tajin btata

MOROCCO

Serves 4

2 lbs. lamb shoulder cut in 8 pieces
2 lbs. small firm potatoes
1 preserved lemon (rind only)
1 dozen bruised green olives
1 tsp. saffron powder
1 tsp. powdered ginger
1 garlic clove, crushed
1 cup vegetable oil
Salt

Sauté the meat in a stew pot. Sprinkle with the salt, saffron, ginger, and garlic. Add water to cover and simmer over low heat, adding more water if necessary.

When the meat is cooked; take it out of the pot. Put the potatoes into the pot with the sauce; cover and simmer until the potatoes are cooked.

Add the sliced rind of the preserved lemon and the olives. Reduce the sauce, add the meat back into the pot and cook for a few more minutes.

Arrange the meat in an attractive serving dish. Add the potatoes, then the lemon slices and the olives. Top with the sauce.

Tadgine with Quince

Tajin sfargel
MOROCCO

Serves 6

2 lbs. quince
2 lbs. lamb shoulder cut into 8 pieces
1 tsp. black pepper
½ tsp. crushed saffron threads
2 small onions
2 tbsp. honey
5 oz. samn *(mix of butter and olive oil) or butter*
Salt

Place the meat in a heavy pot, season with salt, pepper, and saffron, add one sliced onion, and the *samn* or butter. Add water to cover and simmer over medium heat for 50 minutes, stirring occasionally.

Meanwhile, clean, quarter, and remove the seeds from the quince. When the meat is cooked, take it out of the pot, and then add the quince with the remaining sliced onion. Add salt, a little water, and keep an eye on the sauce, remove the pieces of quince as soon as they are cooked.

Stir honey into the sauce, add the meat, then the quince, reheat over low heat.

Arrange the pieces of meat in an attractive serving dish, then add the pieces of quince, and top with the sauce.

The apricot

I HOPE MY ARMENIAN FRIENDS forgive me. Although the apricot's name is *Prunus armeniaca*, its origin is not Armenia, but China. Additionally, another delicious fruit, the peach, that the botanists claim came from Persia, had its origins in China. I hope this won't upset the French: the best apricots are not grown in Roussillon. Of course, they are quite good, but not as good as the fruits of honey and gold found in the East. The apricot tree, which is known for its fastidiousness, seems to have elected Turkey and Syria as its very special residence. It could be said that it found its home in these two countries and grows easily in these safe havens. I even have a feeling that it is the Syrians, and especially the people of Damascus, though they are not generally tempted by metaphysical speculation, who have spread around, if not invented, the legend that Adam and Eve's tree, which was created to teach us how to distinguish between good and evil, is the apricot tree, and not the apple or the fig tree. This would suggest that it is not possible to resist the temptation of the apricot, or else, a clever ploy to locate the Garden of Eden in Syria!

It is imperative to mention that before the ravages of modernization on Damascus, the art of living in that city followed, in some ways, the growing season of the apricot, at least for a few months. As early as in March, the apricot trees in bloom announce the coming of spring. Still today, the apricot regularly attracts a diverse crowd of admirers to the gardens of Ghouta. But, the wonder of the people of Damascus at the delicate beauty of the flowers, with their white corollas enhanced by tender pink hues, is also a matter of concern. Like all early creations, the tender blossoms are subject to the haphazard onslaughts of fate: too heavy a rainfall, too violent a gush of wind, or a late frost. Only the shouts of the street-merchants, when June finally arrives, are likely to reassure the public. Then they can hear the praise of the *mishmish baladi*, the "rose water balls," or the *hamawi* "the flirtatious one," which deserves to be carried "in a silk handkerchief." Thus starts the apricot season, and it is sadly short, after such a long period of waiting. It has inspired an expression in Arabic that describes anything fleeting or improbable. Therefore, when apricot season begins, everyone starts eating them conscientiously, until they can eat no more, for fear they might not have enough the next season. Suddenly, on all the terraces of the city, you can see marmalades and jams in jars of various sizes, exposed to the sun, directly in the air, covered only with a piece of cloth to protect them from dust and insects. The apricot, picked when it is ripe and drenched in light, embodies its Latin denomination, *apricum*, the sunny fruit.

But, the infatuation of our Damascus contemporaries for the apricot pales in comparison to the passion of their ancestors. At the time of the Mameluks, according to the Egyptian traveler Badri, himself an unashamed gourmet, the gardens of Ghouta were producing twenty-one varieties of apricots, only nine of which are known today. And, in order to appreciate them for their true exquisite perfection in beauty and taste, in such a short time, you had to dedicate yourself to each of them, body and soul. The *Ulamas*[1] would not hesitate to take a vacation during the apricot season, abandoning their pulpits and their books at once. In a way, they were abiding by a pleasant custom that had been introduced as early as the mid 13th century C.E. by an august *Gadi*,[2] himself a gardener at times. Sultan Baybar had appointed him to the envied position in Damascus. This season was blessed in many ways, for the muses were also called in to play, and they inspired the scholars with some of their most frivolous metaphors. Apparently, the only element missing was the apricot "wine,"

[1]Theologians and scholars dedicated to the interpretation of Muslim law from a study of the Koran

[2]A Muslim judge

mentioned once by Isfanhani in his Book of Songs. According to him, the musician Ishaq al-Mawsili was crazy about it.

Nowadays no "wine" or liqueur is produced from the apricot. And some of its less problematic uses, such as *mishmishiyya*, a stew of apricots and lamb, and many a sweet and sour dish disappeared from the tables of Damascus several centuries ago. Actually, what is today called *mishmishiyya*, is not made with apricots, but, curiously, with fava beans! Still, it is in Damascus and nowhere else that the preserved apricot reaches magnificence. Only the Turkish dried apricots could rival the Syrian *nuqouʿ*. Those are succulent *baladi*, unseeded, flattened and dried in the sun. They are eaten, mostly during the month of *Ramadan*, as *khoshaf*, to quench thirst. As for the *qamar al-din*, literally the "moon of religion," whose name refers to an old Turkish apricot variety that was especially liked by Ibn Battouta, it shall forever remain the exclusive monopoly of Damascus. It is prepared by mashing the unseeded apricots, then spreading the paste on six-foot long wooden boards, leaving it to dry in the sun. Once the apricot paste is dry, it is brushed with sesame oil, so that it may keep its brilliance and softness, and then folded like a carpet. It is eaten as it is, or better still, soaked in cold water.

In the French marketplace, you can find *qamar al-din* from Syria in the Eastern specialty shops, but you can't find *nuqouʿ*, dried apricots, unless you are ready to settle for the Turkish variety. There are two kinds. One is light colored, sour and treated with sulphur, and I would advise you to avoid it. The other is fleshy and dark in color, a true marvel. When you eat it, you will enjoy its muscatel taste and take advantage of its many benefits, in particular its capacity as a memory booster. All this should not stop you from eating fresh apricots. They have the same nutritive value, provided they were left to ripen on the tree. This obviously

precludes all imported apricots, which are kept in cold storage before they are ripe, depriving them of their taste and smell. Do not resist stewed apricots and jams: they are excellent and the fruits are quite suitable, particularly in France. The height of refinement, once the apricots are cooked, is to remove the almond-shape seeds from inside the pits and add them, scalded and peeled, to the jam. If you are worried about your weight, especially in summer, remember that when the apricot is consumed in this manner, it is the richest fruit in vitamin A. This means that in the process, it helps one get a suntan . . .

Apricot Stew

Marqit mishmish

TUNISIA

Serves 4

1½ lbs. deboned lamb shoulder
1½ lbs. pitted dried apricots
½ cup olive oil
1 tsp. cinnamon
2 rosebuds crushed
2 tbsp. sugar
Salt

Cut the meat into 8 pieces, season with salt, cinnamon, and the crushed rosebuds. Sauté this mixture in the oil, then add water to cover and bring to a boil. Reduce heat, cover, and simmer for 30 minutes.

Add the apricots and sugar, check the seasoning. Simmer another 30 minutes.

Before serving, thicken the sauce by reducing a little.

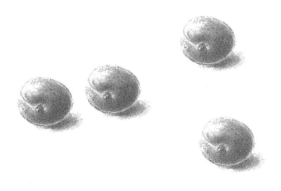

Dried Apricot Dessert

Khoshaf

SYRIA

Serves 6

½ lb. pitted dried apricots
1 lb. seedless raisins
½ cup granulated sugar
1 tbsp. rose flower water
2 tbsp. orange flower water
2½ cups water to soak the raisins and apricots
1 cup mix of crushed almonds, peeled pistachios, pine nuts,
and walnuts

Rinse the raisins and dried apricots and soak them overnight. Drain.

Mix them with the sugar, rose water, and orange water.

Chill. Just before serving *khoshaf*, stir in the other ingredients.

Stewed Apricot Dessert

Mhallabiyet qamar al-din

SYRIA

Serves 6

1 lb. qamar al-din *apricots*
3 cups water
2 tbsp. cornstarch
½ cup water
1 cup sugar
½ cup walnut halves or pine nuts

Soak the *qamar al-din* apricots in water for 8 hours, then mix in the sugar and stir vigorously to dissolve into the fruit.

Put the fruit mixture into a pot and add the cornstarch diluted in water, stir.

Place the pot over medium heat and stir until it boils. Remove from the heat.

Add the walnuts or pine nuts.

Serve chilled.

Wheat Soup Dessert
Barbâra
PALESTINE

Serves 6

1⅛ cup hulled bulgur wheat
½ cup raisins
1 cup qamar al-din (apricot paste)
½ cup sugar
1 tsp. ground fennel seeds
½ tsp. anise
1 cinnamon stick
1 cup chopped walnuts
¾ cup blanched almonds

Cut the apricot paste into small squares and soak for 2 hours in 3 cups of water.

Cook the *bulgur* in four times its volume of water with the fennel, anise, and cinnamon. While the mixture is cooking, add the raisins, sugar, and a little water if necessary.

Mash the apricot/water mixture with a fork and stir until you get a homogenous paste. Strain it into the pot with the other ingredients and stir.

Once the *bulgur* is cooked, pour the mixture into bowls, sprinkle with nuts and almonds, and serve hot.

The olive

POLITICAL SCIENTISTS WILL one day admit that what brings us Mediterranean people together is not, or not yet, the pursuit of common interests or nostalgia for a more or less hypothetical Golden Age, but the definite, absolute conviction that there is only one oil, olive oil. This is anchored deep in every one of us. It is a matter of taste, and this should not hurt anybody's feelings, not even the most fervent worshippers of butter. As a matter of fact, "the Mediterranean" starts and ends where the olive trees grow. The olive is more necessary in our landscape than wheat, or the grapevine. Everybody knows that our people, at least those living along the Eastern shores, have always lived among the olive trees. They made it a symbol for all the things they held dear, starting with fertility, peace and glory. They never stopped competing for the honor of having been the first to use it. According to the Egyptians, it was Isis, the sister and wife of Osiris, who taught humans how to grow olive trees and the art of extracting the oil. The Greeks bestowed the honor on Athena, the protector of arts and sciences. They explained that by growing the first olive tree, she obtained from the assembly of the gods the lordship over both Attica and the city that was to become so glorious as to bear her very name. But the Cretans claimed the merit too—and they have a weighty argument, not only figuratively speaking, thanks to the giant amphoras that were found in the palace at Knossos.

I will not intervene in that debate, though it is almost certain today that the olive tree first grew on the Eastern shore of the Mediterranean about six thousand years ago. I will let others explain how it reached Egypt, then Greece and North Africa, before it ended up somewhat later in Italy and in Provence. To encompass geography, history, economics and the legend of the olive tree would require large volumes. There are quite a few good stories in French, and they would be remarkable, were it not for the ridiculously small segments dedicated to the Arabs. It so happens that, regardless of religion or traditions, the Arabs have always paid homage to the miraculous tree and entrusted it with unparalleled symbolism. In the Koran, God swears by the olive tree, associating it with Mount Sinai, and mentions it in several places as the sign of His infinite goodness. The tree is also mentioned to represent divine Light, a "blessed tree, an olive tree which is neither from the East nor from the West; fire hardly needs to touch it to light up its divine oil." It is indeed a central tree. Muslim esotericism sees in it a figure of universal Man, a Prophet or an Imam, it is linked to Abraham himself, and a product of his hospitality. Many popular beliefs were added later, and some of them are still around. They perpetuate the very old veneration for the oil, which served as a holy unction.

But, let us return to more gastronomical preoccupations. While they do not consume as much oil as the Greeks, the world champions in the matter, the Mediterranean Arabs are actually among the rare people who know how to use it. This is evidenced by the great number of Maghreb dishes, and in particular the succulent Moroccan *tadjine* with cardoons, which was cooked to assess the quality of the new oil, or the authentic Lebanese *mezze*, which is far better than anything made under the same name anywhere else in the East. There was a time when almost everywhere, from Al-Andalus to Palestine, people strove to produce a quality oil, fruity, sweet, or "in between the two," depending on their tastes. To obtain these delicate differences, they handpicked the olives one by one, making sure that they were equally ripe and all the same size. The olive oil that was most sought after, in Spain as well as in Iraq, appears to have been the *unfaq*, the worthy heir of the famous *omphacine* of the Romans. To my knowledge, it is not produced any where in the world today. It was made with unripened, green olives, was particularly translucent and somewhat bitter. Today, in the mills of some producers, you can taste an oil that is even more splendid, but they keep it for their own consumption. It is drawn before the paste of crushed olives is even pressed. Thank God, if you are crazy about olive oil, that is not the only way to enjoy it. You can run across a good bottle every day, as you will with wine, from Kabilya[1] or Lebanon, Sfax in Tunisia or Safita in Syria. But my Arab patriotism will not stop me from writing that I consider some French oil products from around Aix-en-Provence as the very best. They are made with a special variety of olives, the "Saurine."[2] I love tasting the oil as it is, dipping a piece of garlic bread, or else with za'tar, a special thyme that grows in the East.

Just like the oil, whose techniques of extraction have hardly varied over the centuries, table olives are prepared in the same way almost everywhere. The green ones are picked in the fall before they are ripe, and must be treated against bitterness, either by dipping them in a lye-based solution before rinsing and leaving them in brine, or by just leaving them in water long enough and changing the water numerous times. This second method is less popular, and people generally break the olives open before they treat them against bitterness with cold water. They are then kept in salt water and usually seasoned with fennel and coriander seeds. As for black olives, they are picked ripe in the heart of winter. You only have to keep them in brine. But there are several other more sophisticated methods to prepare them. In many Arab countries, they are preserved in salt, then washed, sun dried and kept in oil. In France everyone is familiar with the Greek *kalamata*, which is prepared by adding wine vinegar and oil to the brine. Beside green and black olives, there are the purple ones. The Moroccans have a special approach in their prepara-

---

[1]Kabilya is a region east of Algiers

[2]"Saur" in Provençal means "blond"

tion: they first slit the olives open, then treat them against bitterness with fresh water, and finally, they preserve them in a mixture of water and bitter orange juice. Sometimes they add bergamot, a fragrant lemon. Purple olives are eaten as appetizers, or condiments to add taste to many recipes.

I could talk at length; explain for example what we owe to Spain or to Italy. I could emphasize Tunisia's eminent position; relate Kabylia's traditions, which are so rich and so touching. But, it would be too long. Let my readers remember that olive oil is not merely food: according to many physicians, it is some kind of a miracle medicine. It protects the digestive tracts, regulates glycemia, and eliminates bad cholesterol. Finally, when used by women after their baths, it makes their skin even softer. The only problem is, they may slip away from you!

Garlic Sauce

Salset tum

MIDDLE EAST

Serves 4

1 large potato
1 head of garlic
½ lemon
1 slice whole wheat bread, soaked in water
½ cup olive oil
Salt and pepper

Boil the potato, then mash it.

Bake the garlic head for 10 minutes, peel and crush the cloves, and add to the mashed potato.

Add the lemon juice, squeeze the water from the bread, add with salt and pepper to the potato mixture.

Stir with a wooden spoon, dribble in the olive oil, until you get a thick consistency.

Serve with barbecued or fried chicken.

Spinach with Olives

Sabnakh bil-zitun

ALGERIA

Serves 6

2 lbs. spinach
½ lb. blanched purple olives
4 tbsp. olive oil
1 tbsp. tomato paste
1 lemon, juice only
1 tsp. powdered cumin
1 pinch paprika
Salt and pepper

Wash and chop the spinach, then cook it in ½ cup of salted water, and drain well.

Sauté the garlic cloves in the oil, add the tomato paste, which you dilute in a little water, the spices, and a pinch of salt. Simmer a few minutes over low heat.

Add the spinach, blanched olives (cooked in boiling water for 2 minutes), and lemon juice, mix and simmer over low heat for 10 minutes, stirring occasionally.

Serve hot or cold.

Chicken with Olives

Djej b-zitun

MOROCCO

Serves 6

1 large farm chicken cut in 8 pieces
1 lb. bruised, fresh, uncured olives (bruise them with a hammer,
without breaking the pits)
1 cup olive oil
1 ripe tomato
1 onion
1 clove garlic
1 tsp. ginger
½ tsp. powdered saffron
½ tsp. cumin
½ tsp. black pepper
1 tsp. paprika
½ lemon, juice only
Cilantro and parsley
Salt

Pit the olives and boil them three times for 2 minutes, changing
the water each time. Drain and set aside.

Sprinkle the pieces of the chicken with the salt and spices, then
sauté the chicken in oil with the crushed garlic and chopped
onion. Add water to cover, cover the mixture with a lid, and simmer, stirring occasionally. While the mixture is cooking, add the
peeled, seeded, diced tomato and a tablespoon each of chopped
parsley and cilantro. If necessary, add a little more water.

Just before serving, add the olives, pour in the lemon juice, and
give the mixture a stir. Check the seasoning and boil one minute.
Arrange the chicken in an attractive serving dish, top with the
olives and then with the sauce.

Stuffed Olive Stew

Marqit zitun

TUNISIA

Serves 4

1 lb. ground meat
½ lb. pitted green olives
1 onion
1 cup parsley
1 egg
1 cup olive oil
2 tbsp. tomato paste
1 tsp. paprika
1 tsp. tabil *(a mixture of coriander, caraway, garlic, hot pepper)*
Salt and pepper

Mix the meat well with the onion and the finely chopped parsley, egg, *tabil*, salt and pepper. Fill the olives with this stuffing.

Pour the olive oil into a pot and add the tomato paste, paprika, and 1½ cups water. Add a little salt and bring to a boil.

Add in the stuffed olives and simmer over very low heat for 10 minutes.

The date

W E HAVE TO ACKNOWLEDGE that we owe a lot to the eminent scientists who, after a long and complicated research on fossils, have succeeded in proving that the date tree, or more precisely its ancestor, the wild palm tree, was born in an area around Paris. If it were to be adequately publicized, this amazing discovery might incite the French to eat more dates. This would be a good thing for our Public Health Programs. It would also be good for our Tunisian and Algerian brothers!

In lieu of those austere excavation reports, I tend to prefer our popular legends, and fortunately there are plenty of them. According to the savoriest one, authenticated by a *hadith*[1] of the Prophet, God created the date tree out of the same clay he used to make Adam. Therefore, the date tree has a special significance everywhere in the Islamic countries. It is closer to humans than any other tree: inasmuch as it could be their uncle—or better yet, their aunt on their father's side. It is mentioned several times as a saying of the Prophet himself. By saying this, though much more affectionately, the Muslims were only acknowledging the heritage of the ancient civilizations of the Near East. These ancient civilizations were the first to tame the date-palm tree, first in Mesopotamia, where we find the oldest and most incredible reference, dating back three thousand years, i.e., two

[1]Narrative record of the sayings of Muhammad

thousand years before the Bible. I am thinking of one cylindrical seal, which rather amazingly represents the scene of original sin: on the left, there is a man, on the right, a woman and a serpent, and in the center a magnificent date tree.

Whereas it was a holy tree for the Sumerians and later for the Assyro-Babylonians, the date tree was the tree of life for the Egyptians. They named it *bennou*, the bird that is born every day, like the rising sun. *Bennou* impressed the Greeks so much that they called it *phoinix*, another fabulous bird that is reborn from its own ashes. The Hebrews made it into the figure of the Just, but they did not abandon its previous symbolism of regeneration, resurrection and immortality, in particular when it came to the palm leaves. This explains why, in the Gospel according to John, the inhabitants of Jerusalem welcomed Jesus as he was entering the Holy City for the last time by waving date-palm leaves. It was an expression of joy as much as the announcement of Christ's impending death and final resurrection.

Therefore, the Arabs have good reasons to honor the date tree as they do. All the more, there were 93 million trees in the world, and 75 million were found in Arab countries, of which 32 million of them grew in Iraq, before the madness of war destroyed so many scores of them. We have to admit that the generally arid or semi-arid Arab countries offer an ideal climate for the date tree. During the six or more months required by the stringing process before the dates are ripe, they have time to be saturated with light, and gradually shed their humidity and astringency, since it hardly rains there. Besides, because they have grown in the area for such a long time, Algeria's or Egypt's, Hedjaz's[2] or Iraqi's palm orchards have had all possible opportunities to diversify and accommodate a considerable number of varieties—and each one has its own particularities. Twelve centuries ago, only in the area around Basra, Jahiz counted 360 varieties! And it is almost impossible today to know the names and characteristics of the dozens, or hundreds of varieties in every country, unless you wish to ded-

[2]Saudi Arabia

icate yourself totally to such a study. And yet, the date tree, like everything in this world, is subjected to the harsh law of capitalism. Sooner or later, it will be subjected to the yoke of selection and standardization.

This is why I will only mention a dozen names of date trees, and I will start with the most famous, at least in France: the *Deglet Nour*. Allegedly, it refers to a princess, who in the late 13th century C.E. planted the seeds in the orchard of Al-Harira, not far from Touggourt, in Algeria. Three centuries later, a planter from Tozeur introduced the *Deglet Nour* in Tunisia, where it thrived. Although they are not so delicate, Algeria's *Ghars* and *Degla beida* must not be ignored—the former is soft, the latter dry. Nor should we ignore Tunisia's delicate, *'Allig*, which is primarily used in pastries. The Egyptians will tell you that their *Zaghloul* and *Sammani* are unrivaled. These dates make an excellent jam, flavored with cloves, but they are so sweet that you can eat them green. The Saudis claim that al-Ahsa's dates, like the *Hulas* and the *Ruzeiz*, are better than all others, and Medina maintains the same, even more so. The people of Medina have a point there, with their *'Anbara, Chalabi*, and their *Hulwa*, the Beautiful One, which can be eaten green, fresh or ripe, and always with the same enjoyment. However, the pilgrims prefer the *'Ajwa*, not only because its taste is delicious, but also because it is produced by a date tree which the Prophet supposedly planted himself. All this is true, but Iraq has the most convincing arguments as Iraq's production of *Hallawi* and *Khadrawi* dates is so varied, and the quality is so good! These dates were their number one export, but they cannot be found anymore, even in the countries where people are crazy for them. Where are the *Barhi* and *Huweiz*, which for us as children were the taste of happiness?

I do not have enough room here to say all the good things I have to say about other varieties, but I cannot hide my admiration for the dates of Tafilalet in Morocco, which some consider the best in the whole Maghreb. In any case, between Mauritania and the Gulf, the palm tree orchards will always be a source of pleasant surprises. In these countries, the date tree is the symbol of a whole civilization, as is the olive tree a little more to the north. The trunk is used for building walls, the palms stripped of their leaves for furniture, the leaves for baskets, the fibers for ropes, but mostly the fruit can be enjoyed as it is, fresh or ripe. However, there are also one thousand ways of preparing it: preserved or stuffed in doughnuts, cookies, tortillas, crackers or nougats. In Iraq, people even use them in typical British cakes, puddings and toffees.

Other uses are very popular in Maghreb cuisines. I am thinking, for instance, of Constantine's *mesfouf* or Tunisia's *rfisa*, which are sweet *couscous* dishes, and of various *tadjines* and stews with lamb, veal and fowl. In Iraq and the Gulf countries, the dates are prepared in various ways, from the simplest, an omelet for example, to the most sophisticated, such as Mossul's *kebbe*, which is prepared with figs and date molasses. You will find following a much easier recipe: *mhammar*, which uses date molasses. It is very popular among pearl fishermen.

Finally, let us have a special thought for two other gifts of the date tree: its "heart," which the amateurs eat raw or cooked, salted or sweetened, and its sap which people used to drink quite a lot, especially the fermented kind. Let us not forget the date "wine," which used to be flavored with cinnamon and cloves, or date liqueur, which today is flavored with anise in the Near Eastern fashion. If you are lucky enough to find it, allow yourself to be tempted and dream away, like the great Iraqi poet Sayyab said of a beautiful woman with green eyes, "like two date trees at dawn."

Rice with Date Molasses

Mhammar

ARABIC GULF

Serves 4

2 cups basmati rice
½ cup date molasses
½ tsp. powdered saffron
½ tbsp. ground cardamom
2 tsp. rose water
1 tsp. salt
2 tbsp. samn *(mix of butter and olive oil) or butter*
6 cups water

Mix the saffron, cardamom, and rose water.

Rinse the rice several times in cold water. Bring the 6 cups of water to a boil, add salt and the rice, and cook uncovered for 8 minutes, then drain.

Add the date molasses to the rice and mix well with a fork.

Heat the *samn*, add the rice mixture to it, then pour in the saffron mixture.

Make a few wells in the rice with a wooden spoon, cover the pot with a clean dishtowel, then seal the pot by covering it with a lid.

Cook over very low heat for 20 minutes.

Serve with grilled fish or lamb.

Lamb Tadgine with Dates

Tajin b-tmer

MOROCCO

Serves 6

2¼ lbs. lamb shoulder, cut in 8 pieces
1 lb. dates
1 tbsp. toasted sesame seeds
¾ cup blanched almonds
1 tsp. ground pepper
1 tsp. powdered saffron
1 cinnamon stick
2 minced onions
8 tbsp. butter
1 tsp. ground cinnamon
2 tbsp. honey

Place the meat in a pot. Add the onions, pepper, saffron, cinnamon stick, and butter. Add water to cover and simmer over medium heat. Stir occasionally, add more water if necessary.

When the meat is almost done, add the powdered cinnamon and honey, turn the meat over in the pot so that it will absorb the flavors.

Remove the meat from the pot. Add the dates and some water if needed to the pot and simmer 5–10 minutes.

Put the meat carefully back into the pot.

Remove from the heat when the sauce thickens to a syrupy texture.

Just before serving, reheat the mixture over low heat. Sauté the almonds in oil. Arrange the meat on an attractive serving plate; cover it with dates, sprinkle with almonds and sesame seeds. Top with the sauce and serve.

Lamb with Stuffed Dates

Bussu la tmessu

ALGERIA

Serves 6

2 lbs. deboned lamb shoulder
1 lb. dates
1 onion
1 tbsp sugar
2 tbsp. samn (mix of butter and olive oil)
½ tsp. salt
½ tsp. turmeric

For the stuffing:
1 cup blanched, ground almonds
½ cup sugar
1 egg
¼ cup orange flower water

Cut the meat in 6 pieces and place it in a pot with the onion cut in half, the *samn*, salt, and turmeric. Add water to cover, stir, simmer over low heat. When the meat is well cooked, add the sugar, stir and remove the pot from the heat.

While the meat is cooking, halve and pit the dates, then prepare the stuffing by mixing the ground almonds, sugar, egg, and orange flower water. Stuff the dates with this mixture and add them carefully to the meat.

Simmer another 10 minutes.

Date Cake

Tamr hulw

IRAQ

Serves 6

1 lb. pitted dates
2 tbsp. samn *(mixture of butter and olive oil)*
2 cups chopped walnuts
2 tbsp. toasted sesame seeds

Pit the dates and simmer them over low heat in the *samn.*

Pack half the dates into an 8 inch square baking dish. Sprinkle the nuts on top and cover with another layer of dates. Press down and even out the mixture in the baking dish.

Sprinkle with sesame seeds and press down with your hand. Chill. Once the dish is cold, the cake may be cut into rectangles or into squares. Store in a sealed container.

Date "Logs"

Rfis tmer

ALGERIA

Serves 6

1 lb. pitted dates
1 lb. medium grain semolina
4 oz. samn *(mix of butter and olive oil) or butter*
1 tbsp. honey

Knead the dates for a long time into a large compact ball.

Brown the semolina in a frying pan without any liquid, then carefully knead in the dates, *samn* or softened butter, and honey.

Roll into balls the size of a walnut and flatten the balls, then shape them into logs.

Fresh Date Jam

Mrabba al-balah

LEBANON

Serves 6

2 lbs. fresh dates
1 cup blanched almonds
2½ cups sugar
10 cloves
Juice of 3 lemons
1 tbsp. grated tangerine rind

Peel the dates and boil them in 2 quarts of water for 30 minutes. Seed them and put a shelled almond inside each date.

Pour half of the sugar into a cooking pot, then place the dates on top and cover with the rest of the sugar, cloves, and grated tangerine rind. Let the mixture sit overnight.

Remove the dates and boil the juice produced in the mixture during the night. Add the juice of 3 lemons, and 5 minutes later add the stuffed dates. Cook and reduce.

The squash

THE SQUASH HAS a bad reputation, at least in France, where its various names like "gourde" ou "citrouille" refer to dumb people, if not worse. Could it be because, once emptied of its seeds, this large vegetable looks like the swollen and hollow head of a human being? Or is this, as a recently published book claims, some kind of a curse brought about by rather weird innuendoes concerning the name of the cucurbit species? The debate on that issue remains inconclusive. But there is one thing we can be sure of about the squash: apparently, refusing to eat it is no guarantee of becoming intelligent!

The people in the East are quite aware of this. They are far from perfect, but at least they have been less cruel with the squash. In the Far East, it was even a symbol of plenty and fertility. Its seeds, which were eaten at the time of the spring equinox, were considered food for immortality. This might have been the case in other countries too. As far as the Near East is concerned, the most popular cucurbit in Antiquity seems to have been the cucumber. The squash was not unknown, though, even in pre-Islamic Arabia. Shortly before Muhammad's Revelation, the poet Imru' l-Qays mentioned it not as food, to be sure, but to evoke the perfect softness of his horse's nose. Islam was the force that gave the squash its title of nobility: it is written in the Koran that after Jonah had been swallowed up into the belly of the whale, then spit out "in a pitiful state on the empty beach," the Lord ordered the *yaqtin*, a plant with large leaves, to spread itself over Jonah. This noun, *yaqtin*, originally applied to all creeping plants, but it was eventually reserved for the squash only, as can be seen today in Eastern Arabic. The Prophet himself is said to have condoned this interpretation. He called the squash "my brother Jonah's shrub." It is known far and wide by various testimonies—one being the testimony of his wife, A'isha—that he was crazy about the *yaqtin*, and that he urged the Muslims to eat it, because, according to him, it had the power "to fortify our hearts when we are sad . . ."

What kind of a squash was it anyway? The question makes sense, since the squash is a most diversified vegetable. There are many species and a considerable amount of varieties, from the small zucchini to the majestic turbaned squash. Some of them are long. Some are spherical. Others are flat, concave or thin in the middle. Their rind is smooth or covered with warts. Their color is creamy or dark green, yellow or red, plain or striped. Many come from America, such as the zucchini, unknown in medieval Near East. Arab agronomists and botanists of the classical age mention many, but with so few details, it is impossible for us to decide what their subspecies were. Still, we may claim that the Arabs knew the so-called "Pilgrim's gourd." Its bottle shape, and more or less long neck are the reasons why the lower part of the squash is still called *qar'a*, or squash. The Arabs, very possibly, grew enough musk squash and several varieties of pumpkins to develop quite an elaborate cuisine. On that account, the cookbooks, that have weathered the centuries, are very different from those in Europe at the same time. While Baghdadi (1226 C.E.) or Ibn al-'Adim (d.1262 C.E.) offered a myriad of recipes for *qar'*, the cookbooks in Europe only mentioned three out of 2,274 recipes. Besides, these paltry entries dealt with all the squash varieties, not one in particular. The disinterest for the squash in Europe is responsible for its quasi absence, but we must not forget that vegetables were generally despised in the West until the Renaissance.

Thank heaven that times have changed! Today, both sides of the Mediterranean are competing for new ways to honor vegetables, even if, in this, the Arabs apparently still have the upper hand. If you are not so sure, may I suggest

Morocco's lamb (or chicken) *tadjine* with mashed pumpkin? It is caramelized and flavored with cinnamon. The Algerians use another squash, but their recipe is almost identical, except that they add a spoon of orange flower water to the purée. And, in the three countries in Maghreb, couscous dishes with red squashes cooked with one or several vegetables, like the famous *bidaoui*, are very popular. There is a couscous dish in Tunisia with squash and green fava beans. I was lucky enough to try another remarkable Moroccan dish. It is made with dried beef—*khli*—and lentils, onions, peeled and seeded tomatoes, and some red squash with a very hot green pepper. In the Near East, particularly in Syria, two dishes are especially interesting: one with pumpkin and chickpeas and a lamb shank, the other with pumpkin and peas, the juice of one lemon, sesame cream, and ground meat. They may be served with rice, but they are much better with cracked wheat. The combination of wheat and squash is always a success. You should try the pumpkin *kebbe*, which the Christians in Syria and Lebanon invented for Lent.

In addition to the pumpkin, the zucchini is quite necessary for our culinary enjoyment. It has in Arab cuisine a position that is very possibly unique in the world. I am thinking in particular of five dishes of stuffed zucchinis, which are among the masterpieces of Syrian-Lebanese cuisine. They are quite easy to make, except for the part where the insides have to be scooped out. There is not enough room here, so I have written only one of the recipes below. The four others are quite as splendid, with different stuffings (meat and rice, meat and pine nuts, rice and onions) and different liquids to cook them in (tomato or tamarind juice, or fermented milk). You can also enjoy zucchini starters, salads, purées and omelets, and various stews too. The most amazing recipe in Maghreb is an Algerian recipe for white zucchini jam. You would have thought it came from England. But, there are two Moroccan dishes that I believe are even better: zucchinis with *khli* and gumbos, and couscous with zucchinis, fresh fava beans and turnips, flavored with cilantro. The Moroccans also have an intelligent way of using the gourd-shaped zucchini. They call it *slaouia*, but it looks like the *yaqtin* in the East. Like its Near Eastern cousin, it adds a special note of taste to a salad, *tadjine* or stew. The street merchants in Damascus will tell you that eating it will cure you of all your ills.

I have a great friend in Nice who is bound to ask me, what about the zucchini flower? He once blamed me for preferring the olive oil from Les-Baux-de-Provence to his local variety. I must say that I am sensitive to the question, because fried zucchini flowers are one of the two vegetable dishes of the French of which I am most envious. Is there indeed a subtler dish than these yellow flowers? They are washed in cold water, dipped in a batter, and then fried. A second dish is even more delicious. Imagine a whole pumpkin. It has been baking for two hours. Inside, there are alternating layers of toasted bread spread with garlic paste, button mushrooms, and grated Savoie cheese and crème fraîche. The pulp has then been delicately mixed with all the other ingredients, and the entire pumpkin is presented whole in its majesty in the middle of the table. I am sure that even if you are indifferent to fairy tales, you will think that you are in Cinderella's coach.

Purée of Pumpkin

Yaqtin mtabbal

SYRIA

Serves 6

2 lbs. fresh pumpkin
3 garlic cloves
¾ cup tahini *(sesame paste)*
Juice of 2 lemons
Parsley
1 tsp. ground cumin
Salt

Dice the pumpkin and boil for 30 minutes in 1 cup of water.

Drain well, purée the pumpkin, add the *tahini* and mix.

Crush the garlic with salt, mix in the lemon juice, and stir this mixture into the purée.

Sprinkle with ground cumin and finely chopped parsley. Serve.

Stuffed Zucchini

Kussa mahchi

NEAR EAST

Serves 6

12 small zucchinis
1 lb. ground lamb shoulder
1 cup round rice
4 cups tomato juice
1 cup peeled seeded, chopped tomatoes
Juice of a 4 oz. tamarind, which has been soaked in hot water
Crushed garlic, dried mint leaves, salt, pepper,
safflower or powdered cumin

Cut off the ends of the zucchinis and scoop out the zucchini pulp with a *naqqara* or any other adequate utensil, like a very long thin knife. Prepare the stuffing: wash the rice several times in cold water, add the meat, the chopped tomatoes, safflower or cumin, salt and pepper; mix well.

Stuff the zucchinis three fourths full.

Boil the tomato juice and the strained tamarind juice. Season with salt.

Place the zucchinis next to each other and close together in the pot, cover, and cook 30 minutes over low heat.

Add the crushed garlic and the mint, and simmer another 5 minutes, uncovered.

Note: With the zucchini pulp, you can make zucchini fritters and omelets, or a delicious starter with onions, olive oil, garlic, and ground cumin.

Pumpkin Kebbe

Kebbe jlant

LEBANON

Serves 6

2 lbs. fresh pumpkin, peeled and diced
1 cup of fine bulgur *wheat*
2 tbsp. flour
½ cup dried chickpeas, soaked and peeled
2 onions, finely chopped
Fresh mint, finely chopped
Paprika, hot pepper, cinnamon
Oil, salt, sugar

Boil the pumpkin for 15 minutes. Drain and purée it.

Mix the pumpkin with the *bulgur* in a large pot. Let it set for a while to blend.

Then add in the flour, onion, fresh mint, spices, and salt. Knead, add the chickpeas, and mix everything together well.

Spread this paste evenly in an oiled baking dish and make a pattern by cutting through the paste, first into quarters, then cut pie shapes in each quarter. Next cut each pie piece into three parts.

Sprinkle with sugar and oil, then put the *kebbe* in a preheated oven.

Bake at 350°F for 40 minutes.

Tadgine with Pumpkin

Tajin b-qa'ra hamra

MOROCCO

Serves 8

9 lbs. fresh pumpkin, peeled and cut in thin slices
3½ lbs. lamb shoulder, cut into 8 pieces
1 cup sugar
1 cup olive oil
1 garlic clove
½ tsp. saffron powder
½ tsp. ginger
1 tsp. cinnamon
½ tsp. flour
1 tsp. toasted sesame seeds
½ cup blanched almonds
Salt

Place the meat in a heavy pot, season with the saffron, ginger, crushed garlic and half of the oil. Add salt to taste, cover with water, and simmer covered, stirring occasionally. If necessary, add some water while it cooks.

Mix the flour in a little water and add it to the meat sauce.

Cook the pumpkin without any liquid in a large heavy bottomed or non-stick stew pot, stirring constantly until you get a thick purée. Add the sugar, oil, and a pinch of salt, and keep cooking, stirring constantly in order to caramelize the purée. Mix in the cinnamon and skim off the oil that comes to the top.

Just before serving, reheat the meat and arrange the pieces in an attractive deep serving dish. Pour the mashed pumpkin on top, then the meat sauce, and decorate with the almonds, which have been sautéed in oil to a golden color, and finally sprinkle the sesame seeds over the top.

Omelet, Alexandria Style

'Ujja iskandaraniyya

SYRIA

Serves 6

2 lbs. zucchinis
½ lb. deboned ground lamb shoulder
1 onion
6 eggs
1 cup flour
1 cup chopped parsley
1 tsp. dried mint
1 pinch hot pepper
1 tbsp. baking soda
Salt and pepper
Peanut oil

Slice the zucchinis in rounds and fry them in the oil. Drain, and purée them in a bowl. Sauté the meat with the finely chopped onion. Add the parsley. Mix all ingredients together.

Butter a baking dish, and pour in the mixture evenly, bake in preheated 375°F oven for 15 minutes.

Zucchini Tadgine with Thyme
MOROCCO

Serves 6

2½ lbs. lamb shoulder, cut into 6 pieces
3½ lbs. zucchini
1 chopped onion
3 tbsp. samn *(mix of butter and olive oil)*
1 tbsp. powdered thyme
1 tsp. pepper
½ tsp. saffron
Salt

In a stew pot put the meat, chopped onion, *samn*, pepper, and saffron. Add salt to taste, cover with water, and simmer covered over medium heat, then reduce to low heat.

Meanwhile, cut the zucchinis in thick slices, rub them with thyme and a little salt. When the meat is cooked, remove it from the sauce and then drop the zucchinis into the pot with the sauce. Add 1 cup of water, stir, bring to a boil, and simmer, uncovered over low heat.

Reduce the sauce and put the meat carefully back into the pot. Once the meat is hot, place it in an attractive serving dish, spoon the zucchini over it, and pour the sauce on top.

Zucchini Stew

Mderbel qar'a

ALGERIA

Serves 6

2¼ lbs. zucchinis
2¼ lbs. lamb shoulder, deboned
3 tbsp. butter
3 tbsp. peanut oil
½ cup dried chickpeas, soaked and drained
4 garlic cloves
½ tsp. caraway seeds
½ tsp. cinnamon
1 tbsp. vinegar
Salt and pepper

Cut the zucchinis in thin slices and sauté in 2 tablespoons of oil and 2 tablespoons of butter. Drain on paper towels.

In a heavy pot, melt the remaining butter with 1 tablespoon oil, cut the meat in 6 pieces and add it to the pot, with the crushed garlic, spices, and a little salt. Sauté for 5 minutes, then cover with water, add in the chickpeas, and cook covered over low heat.

Once the meat is cooked, take it out of the pot and drop the zucchini slices into the sauce. Add the vinegar and stir.

Put the meat in an attractive deep serving dish. Top with the zucchini, and pour the sauce over it.

The tomato

I WILL NEVER QUITE get used to the idea that my respected ancestor and master, Abu al-Hasan 'Ali ibn Nafi', a.k.a. Ziryab, who lived in the 9th century C.E. in Baghdad, then in Cordoba, never bit into one tomato in his lifetime, nor even had the opportunity of imagining what a pepper or a potato might look like. The only beneficial gift that the Conquistadors brought back to us when they returned from America are those three marvels of creation, as well as corn and most beans, which only began to be used in the Old World in the early 16th century C.E. The various cuisines along the Mediterranean, including those of the Arab world, are today strongly marked by the taste and color of the tomato. Then, however, and for another three or four centuries, the Mediterranean diet was quite different. This means that at the time when the Aztecs were already producing large quantities of this delicious red berry and making a hot salsa with it in the floating gardens of Tenochtitlan, the Italians, whose craze for spaghetti which dates back to the 14th century, were not able to serve pasta with a Neapolitan or a Bolognese sauce . . .

This is one of the most striking paradoxes in the history of gastronomy and beyond, a fine example of the changeability of human mores evidenced by the following extremely dramatic episode: Whereas the tomato was first compared to the Solanaceous, a magical and poisonous species, today, ketchup, its most debatable by-product, has won universal victory in this end of the century. As soon as it was introduced in Europe, first in Spain, Portugal and then Italy (through the Spanish kingdom of Naples), the tomato was related by the populace to the mandrake, of the deadly nightshade family. This connected it directly

79

to the bewitching figure of Circe.[1] Its supposedly toxic berries were also invested with mysterious powers, an aphrodisiac in particular. This is probably why many European languages called it the "love apple," even though the botanists, who refused the Solanaceous myth, preferred to give it a less attractive name: *Lycopersicum esculentum*, the "wolf peach." Very early on, they remarked on the use of that special peach in the kitchen. As early as in 1544, Petrus Matthiolus wrote that it was cooked like mushrooms, fried in olive oil and seasoned with salt and spices. But, the somewhat murky and naïve beliefs about the tomato were to keep it for a long time in a minor role of decoration or medicine.

This was especially true in France. While Provence and Languedoc seem to have adopted the tomato as a fruit and vegetable very early on, the area around Paris and the North were suspicious of the tomato until the late 18th century. There were no tomatoes in the famous King's kitchen garden in Versailles. We know, through the irrefutable testimony of Brillat-Savarin himself, that the tomato was still very practically unknown in Paris by 1789. It was finally popularized one year later in 1790 because of the Marseilles delegates: In their revolutionary zeal they had traveled up to Paris to take part in the "Fête de la Fédération," and very vigorously and successfully demanded tomatoes on their table. It took even longer in Eastern Europe, where the Church and Synagogue, were concerned about whether it was legitimate to eat the mandrake's relative. One can surmise that what was at stake was the alleged capacity of the tomato to stimulate sexual desire. This fallacious reputation has survived, for example, among some farmers of the Midi. Curiously enough, a few thousand miles to the South, the Bambaras of West Africa seem to have the same conviction. One of their matrimonial rites consists of eating a tomato before sex.

To avoid appearing contemptuous or condescending, I must explain why we Arabs were never tempted to behave that way. Not that we were more confident of our own male prowess, but

---

[1] A sorceress in Homer's *Odyssey*

the tomato came to us from Europe very late in time, in the mid 19th century, when we had become dazzled by the West and didn't know how to question its spell. That is why we were never aware of the similarity between the tomato and the mandrake, although it had troubled the botanists of the classical age, like Ibn al-Baytar, as no other plant ever had.

To my knowledge, the only indication of a possible misgiving about the tomato is to be found in Alep, where the fruit was introduced in 1268/1851. For many years, it was only eaten green, and the women would hide their faces with their veils if they happened to be looking at it. Another sign: it was called *frangi*, "frank," as was everything from Europe, whether a variety of the eggplant, or a venereal disease. But so what? After all, the French called corn "Turkish wheat," because it was not something to be trusted. From that time on, things went fast. The *Description of Egypt* does not say one word about the tomato, but Egypt's economic statistics included it after 1880; it had become an item for export, and was sent to the various European marketplaces during the off-season. Even more significantly, the Bustani family was wise enough to dedicate an article to the tomato in their encyclopedia, *Da'irat al-ma'arif*, even though it had hardly made its debut in Lebanon and Syria. At the same time, a few decades after the French conquest of Algeria, the tomato was heavily produced there. It was first grown in the vegetable farms west of Oran, not far from the Moroccan border. Production then spread over to Algiers, in 1910. When it was introduced in Morocco, the French decided to grow it in the off-season in the area around Rabat and Al-Jadida, then around Agadir (in the 1930s), where it developed the magnificent standing that it has today.

I will not insult my readers by enumerating, even briefly, the multitude of ways to use tomato, for it is undeniably the universal vegetable today. You can find it in sauces and salads, and with many dishes. It is made into juice, jam, and even sorbet with a dash of vodka. It is everywhere, accompanying every kind of meat. It is at its best with mint, basil, pepper, and eggplant, with spaghetti and potatoes, or with olives and ewe cheese. Its real lovers know how to enjoy it just by itself, like this man in Joseph Delteil's *Cholera*, who would eat his tomatoes raw, "heavy like hips," with "their pulp pink like a pubis," only sprinkled with salt, garlic and cloves. The tomato is so kind as to keep its taste when the sun dries it, cut in thin slices and placed on a bed of straw, or as a paste spread onto flat, preferably glass, dishes. In any case, you should know that a canned tomato is always tastier than a tomato that has been grown in the off-season. Such a tomato cannot be ripe and will have no taste, as beautiful as it may look. Two centuries ago, Grimod de la Reynière, the founding father of Western gastronomy, had already said: "Premature pleasures are always, and in everything, imperfect pleasures."

Spicy Tomatoes

Banadora harra

NEAR EAST

Serves 6

2 lbs. ripe tomatoes
4 garlic cloves
1 tsp. cumin
1 tsp. sumac
1 tsp. hot pepper
½ cup olive oil
Salt and pepper

Heat the oil and sauté the thinly sliced garlic cloves. Add the tomatoes, which have been peeled, seeded and diced. Mix and cook over medium heat for 10 minutes. Season with salt, pepper, cumin, sumac, and hot pepper, and simmer 5 more minutes over low heat.

Serve cold with other appetizers (*mezzés*).

Salad with Tomatoes and Peppers

Slada b-matisha wel-felfel

MOROCCO

Serves 6

4½ lbs. very ripe tomatoes
2 green peppers
2 hot peppers (optional)
1 preserved lemon (rind only)
1 cup chopped parsley
½ cup olive oil
1 tsp. paprika
Salt

Crush the garlic together with a little salt and paprika. Peel, seed and chop the tomatoes, then cook the tomatoes and garlic in olive oil over low heat, stirring constantly.

Grill the green peppers and hot peppers, peel and dice them. Chop the lemon rind. Add these ingredients with the parsley to the tomatoes. Mix, salt to taste, and cook 15 more minutes, stirring constantly.

Serve cold.

Stuffed Tomatoes

Yalangi banadora

SYRIA

Serves 6

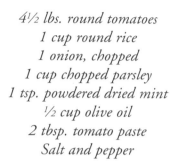

4½ lbs. round tomatoes
1 cup round rice
1 onion, chopped
1 cup chopped parsley
1 tsp. powdered dried mint
½ cup olive oil
2 tbsp. tomato paste
Salt and pepper

Wash the rice many times, drain and sauté it in olive oil with the onion, parsley, mint, paprika, and a pinch of salt and pepper. Gradually add one cup of water and then remove from the heat, as soon as the rice has absorbed all of the liquid.

Cut off the tops of the tomatoes, remove the seeds and part of the pulp with a teaspoon. Fill the tomatoes with the rice stuffing and put the tops back on. Place the tomatoes in an oiled baking dish, sprinkle with tomato sauce (a mixture of the chopped tomato pulp and the tomato paste diluted in 1 cup of water), and bake in a preheated oven (425°F) for 15 minutes.

Serve cold.

Tomato Stew

Mirmiz

TUNISIA

Serves 4

1 lb. lamb
1 lb. tomatoes
2 green peppers
2 hot peppers
2 onions
¼ cup chickpeas
⅓ cup olive oil
½ tsp. tabil (a mixture of coriander, caraway, garlic, hot pepper)
Salt and pepper

Saute the meat in a little olive oil with chopped onions and season with salt, pepper and *tabil.*

Add the chickpeas, which have been soaked overnight, and the peeled, seeded, chopped tomatoes. Sprinkle with the paprika, add water to cover, and cook for 40 minutes over low heat.

Add the hot peppers and green peppers, seeded and cut into strips. Simmer 10 more minutes.

Check the seasoning and serve hot.

Tomato Ragout

Mnazzalet banadora

SYRIA

Serves 6

4 lbs. very ripe tomatoes
1¼ lbs. ground lamb
4 onions, chopped
4 garlic cloves, sliced
¼ cup pine nuts
Samn *(mix of butter and olive oil) or butter*
Salt, pepper, ground cinnamon

Peel, seed, and drain the tomatoes. Then chop them.

In a pan, toast the pine nuts, set aside. Sauté the onions and meat in the *samn* or butter. Add the salt and spices, and cook for another 10 minutes, stirring, occasionally.

Add the garlic and tomatoes. Mix carefully and simmer over low heat for 15 minutes.

Sprinkle the dish with the pine nuts. Serve with basmati rice or *bulgur* wheat.

Note: Of course, the people in Damascus, who love cilantro, sprinkle some on before serving.

Chicken with Caramelized Tomatoes

Djej b-matisha

MOROCCO

Serves 4

4½ lbs. very ripe tomatoes, peeled, seeded and chopped
1 large chicken, cut into 8 pieces
1 chopped onion
3 cloves garlic, chopped
8 tbsp. butter
3 tbsp. honey
1 cup toasted blanched almonds
1 tbsp. toasted sesame seeds
½ tsp. pepper
½ tsp. ginger
½ tsp. saffron
1 tsp. cinnamon powder
Salt

In a heavy pot, place the chicken, tomatoes, butter, onions, garlic, salt, pepper, ginger, saffron, and 1 cup of water. Cook over medium heat for 45 minutes.

Remove the pieces of chicken from the pot, as soon as they are cooked.

Caramelize the tomatoes by stirring them frequently and then add the honey and cinnamon, still stirring.

Place the chicken back in the pot for a few minutes, to give it the flavor of the sauce.

Arrange the chicken in an attractive serving dish, pour the sauce over it, and top with toasted almonds and sesame seeds.

The fig

THANKS TO MY FRIENDS of *Qantara*, I gave myself the right to confess in public my excessive fondness for figs, but M. Clément Serguier has been especially instrumental in making things difficult for me. About one year ago, I had just made up my mind to tell you about the fig tree, when he dedicated one whole book to the subject. And what a book it is, indeed: A sumptuous festival for our senses, an authentic treatise on the fig, ready to delight the most demanding reader. What more can I say? I must acknowledge, right at the outset, that I can say nothing, or hardly anything more about the ancient history of the fig tree, nor the numerous legends about it.

Clément Serguier knows his Bible in its smallest details, starting with the fig leaves that Adam and Eve used to hide their private parts. He also knows everything about the dried fig cakes, which the patriarch Noah took with him on his ark; the basket of fresh figs which King David, as a sign of homage, received from a young maiden; and the fig tree on the road to Bethany, which was condemned by Jesus to no longer bear any fruit—hinting at those who refused Christ's New Covenant. Neither will you be able to find fault with what he has to say about Egypt, more precisely the tree where the cow Hathor received the soul of the departed: The old Egyptians used to deposit presents at the foot of sycamores. From the book, you will also learn that the tree which sheltered Remus and Romulus after they were saved by the she-wolf who suckled them, was a fig tree. By the way, you will find out that the word "sycophant," which means "informer" in Greek, originally meant the guards of Attica's fig tree orchards. Their job was to tell on those who were trying to export the fruit, which was in such general high esteem. And that the snake, which mortally bit Cleopatra as she was coming out of her bath, was hiding in a basket of figs. And how the king of the Persians decided to conquer Athens because he was crazy about figs. You will learn how Cato the censor took out of his toga a few fresh figs, which had allegedly been picked in Africa three days earlier, to convince his peers, before the Roman Senate, that Carthage was not far and had to be destroyed.

Neither will I be able to add anything on the subject of agriculture or botany. M. Serguier is comprehensive, and he explains everything very well. He is very delicate about explaining to us what "caprification" means. True enough, this notion makes us think of the ram, but it has to do with the pollination of the female fig trees. This task is generally completed in July, by a roguish messenger, the fig wasp, sent by the male fig trees. The pollination is a most bizarre operation, and the farmers in the producing countries have known its secrets for centuries. The strange pollination process allows the fig tree to blossom in the early summer, and the caprification process allows us to fully enjoy the figs of the late season. Those picked in August and September are the best. Besides other considerations in the field of natural history, we are told innumerable particulars about the social uses of the fig, especially in France. And to top it all, M. Serguier gives us a myriad of geographical and economic details, which will fully satisfy us "figophiles." No wonder Provence, which has grown figs for so long, stands in such high regard. I must confess to having been very much impressed by his erudition and willingness to glorify the fig in so many domains: historical, anthropological, agronomic, dialectological and literal. There is even a very serious field study in the book. In these conditions, you can understand that it was very hard for me to go any further. There was only one more thing for me to add and Clément Serguier points the way: He once invites "somebody from the old Ottoman empire" to reveal to him the characteristics of the Eastern tradition about the fig tree. True enough, he had the caliphs, viziers and mandarins in mind. But, what can one do if those people have lost their sense of the real life? They are too focused on power and money!

Let us start with the beginning, that is, for the Muslims, with the Koran. The fig is quoted once only, in a Mecca *sura*[1] entitled "the fig." In it, the Lord swears by the fig and the olive, Mount Sinai and "this secure city," by which He means Mecca. Some Muslim exegetes have concluded that the *sura* does not speak of the fig and the olive, but of the cities of Damascus and Jerusalem. According to them, this is justified by the fact that the fig tree, which cannot tolerate being close to the date tree, is not to be found anywhere in Hedjaz. This would explain the absence of the fig in the Muslim tradition. Some consider the *hadith*, in which the Prophet mentions it as a fruit of paradise, as not genuine. But do not get the wrong message! The Muslims eventually granted the fig all the attention it deserves. Actually, thanks to the Koran blessing, the conquered lands, in particular Syria, Egypt, and North Africa, produced it in large quantities. Damascus became more than ever identified with the fig. For those who are not convinced, I say that in the very center of the Byzantine basilica, on which the great mosque of the Umayyads was built, there stood a very beautiful fig tree.

Some day I will dedicate some time to recount in detail what happened then, from the time of the Umayyiads, the initiators of Arab-Muslim gastronomy, to the Ottomans who were as fond of food as the Umayyiads. The Turkish Empire spread more or less over the zone where the fig tree grows. This is a very rich history, and we will see that Alep and its region should not be afraid of competing with Damascus, that Arab medicine had a very high consideration both for the fruit and its precious white sap, which was used to cure calluses and tenderize meat. Caprification was strictly regulated, as shown by a *hisba* treatise of Seville. Neither will I forget its role in superstition, as reported by Nabulusi in the 18th century C.E., or the farmers' sayings concerning the cycle of the seasons, or the city proverbs, which made the fig the symbol of an easy life. I will no doubt have to study what agronomists and gastronomists wrote about the mysterious affinity which

---

[1] A *sura* is a section, or chapter of the Koran.

93

unite the fig and the walnut, as illustrated by a most subtle jam. This jam is my favorite, and it bears the lovely name "gazelle ankle." Neither will I ignore the Eastern varieties, which I will classify according to their shapes, round or pear-shaped, the color of their skins, their pulps, their consistencies, tastes and harvest cycles. And I will insist on an anthology of all the metaphors, which the fig inspired to the poets. I am sure you can guess what they are—the fruit, whole or split, is an obvious reminder of the fleshy lips, breasts, and private parts of the beloved woman. Let us go back to Clément Serguier—from this work, let me borrow André Gide's[2] praise of the fig:

> *Its blossom is folding over itself.*
> *A closed room of matrimony;*
> *No scent to the outside world.*
> *Since nothing escapes,*
> *The smell becomes succulence and taste.*
> *A blossom without beauty, yet a fruit of delights;*
> *A fruit that is but its blossom ripened.*

[2]André Gide, French writer, 1869–1951

Fresh Fig Jam

Mrabba al-tin

SYRIA

2 lbs. fresh figs
2½ cups granulated sugar
2 cups water
2 tbsp. lemon juice

Dissolve the sugar in the water and bring to a boil. Skim the foam off the top and add the figs, which have been washed and dried carefully. Add the lemon juice. Stir carefully and cook for 15 minutes over medium heat. Skim again, and reduce the heat to its lowest temperature possible.

Ten minutes later, remove the figs from the pot, but continue cooking the syrup until it thickens. Remove from the heat. Put the figs back in the syrup and chill the jam before putting it in dry, sterilized jars.

Cover with a layer of paraffin wax, as is customary.

Dried Fig Jam

Mrabba in nashef

LEBANON

2 lbs. chopped dried figs, cut in large pieces
2½ cups granulated sugar
2 cups water
1 cup walnuts, chopped
1 cup toasted sesame seeds
1 tsp. ground green anise
1 tbsp. lemon juice
A pinch powdered gum arabic (pectin)

Dissolve the sugar in the water and bring to a boil. Skim and add the figs and lemon juice. Continue stirring.

When the water has evaporated, remove from the heat and mix in the nuts, sesame seeds, anise, and gum arabic.

Return the mixture to the heat, stirring constantly, until it thickens.

Chill, then pour into jars.

Fig Jam

Ma'jun karmus

TUNISIA

2 lbs. firm figs
2½ cups granulated sugar
Juice of 1 lemon
1 pinch ground cloves
1 cup blanched almonds
1 cup pine nuts
4 cups water

In a heavy bottomed pot, pour the 4 cups of water, lemon juice, sugar, and pinch of ground cloves. Bring to a boil then cook over medium heat for 30 minutes.

Cut the figs in quarters and cook for 30 minutes in the syrup. Remove the figs from the pot and continue cooking the syrup until it thickens.

Toast the almonds in the oven for 2–3 minutes and add them to the syrup with the pine nuts and the figs. Cook 10 more minutes.

Couscous

SOME OF MY MAGHREB women friends, who wished me well, kept repeating something to me over and over again: "Give it up, you don't know anything about couscous, you will never know anything about it anyway. You can talk about rice all you like; you can praise *bulgur* wheat; you can laud Bagdad's bread *panadas* or Istanbul's *burkes*; just forget about our couscous." One of them even went so far as to hope I would not get my wheels stuck in the grains, as I would drown in the broth!

It so happens that my name is Ziryab: This means that when dealing with the relations between Mashreq and Maghreb,[1] nobody can presume to tell me what to believe. I am basically convinced that, beyond the obvious political divisions, there was never a break between Damascus or Cairo at one end, and Tunis or Cordoba at the other—not in affairs of gastronomy, not in music, not in literature. In the 13th century C.E., when *kuskusu* had just imposed itself in the lands of Western Islam, Ibn al-'Adim in Alep was already in a position to write about it quite honorably. He wrote no less than four couscous recipes in his cookbook. He attributed one of them, the best obviously, to Maghreb. He not only insisted on the art of rolling the grains, but also on the assurance that the steaming process was perfect. The two parts of the couscous pan, in particular, were to be sealed tight. Over the years, Ibn al-'Adim's couscous disappeared from Syria's tables, but another from Maghreb replaced it: Its name was *moghrabiyya*, and sometimes *kuskusun*. It looked like today's large grain *mhammas*. Maqqari, the famous historian of

[1]The Arabic terms for the Near East, and North Africa

Muslim Spain, was probably speaking of *moghrabiyya* in his famous story where the Prophet Muhammad appeared in a dream to an Eastern scholar. Muhammad advised him to treat his Maghreb guest to a *kuskusun*, because the Maghrebi was nostalgic for his country. People in Egypt also knew how to cook this dish, though in various forms. The most curious of these is *saksakiyya*, a kind of chopped, steamed dough, which Jacques Berque discovered one day in a small village. Supposedly Hilali nomads brought it from Tunisia to Higher Egypt in the 12th century C.E. The Fatimids had expelled them two centuries earlier. I mention this to explain that the Eastern Arabs were not totally unaware of *couscous*. It was probably just another variety of *tharid* for them, as it was for the Maghrebis and the Andalusians, a dish they had always been fond of: a combination of bread crumbs, meat broth, and vegetables. According to a *hadith* believed to be authentic, the prophet himself, who was crazy about it, said that bread *panada* was to all dishes what his beloved wife A'isha was to all women . . .

At this point, and against my own will, I must debunk one very old legend. No, indeed, couscous is not as old as it is generally believed to be, even though the steaming technique goes back to ancient times. A couscous, worthy of this name, must be made with durum wheat, which comes from Ethiopia, and, very likely, was only introduced in Maghreb in the 10th century C.E. From there, it crossed the Straits of Gibraltar to end up in Spain. No wonder there is no mention whatsoever of couscous in Ishaq ibn Sulayman's famous *Book of Food*. Ishaq ibn Sulayman, a Jewish physician and dietician, died in 932 C.E. He lived in Kairouan and was very interested in wheat and its by-products. Actually, we have no mention of couscous in Tunisia during the whole Zirid period until the mid 12th century C.E., nor during the Almohad period that followed. The first reference was found at the time of the first Hafcids (1228–1574 C.E.). As far as Spain is concerned, the precious rolled semolina was equally unknown, either at the time of the caliphs in Cordoba, or under the *reyes de taifas*, although it was already very popular during the period of the last Almohads and in Morocco (in the 13th century C.E.) and their Nasrid successors, who were lucky enough to use a new, excellent durum wheat. Two treatises on cuisine, written by Ibn Razin in Murcia, and an anonymous author who lived about the same time, testified to the new importance of couscous in the diet of Islam's Far West. In the first book, besides the usual recipe with various vegetables (turnips, carrots, fresh fava beans, eggplants, zucchini, etc.), there was a couscous with crushed walnuts, another one with dried fava beans, and an amazing one with a piece of lamb stuffed with couscous and baked. In the second book, couscous was intelligently classified among the bread *panadas*. The book mentions the recipe for a stew seasoned with garlic, vinegar, saffron and cumin, which can be accompanied either with breadcrumbs or semolina.

Couscous is thus a "soup," in the old sense of the word, as Jean-François Revel, who is definitely better inspired in matters of gastronomy than politics, rightfully noted. On the one hand, it is composed of the couscous itself, i.e., the grains, must be light, regular, and loose, but soaked with the juices and fragrances of the stew. On the other hand, you need a lot of skill and patience to succeed in making the couscous grains. You first have to roll some semolina and some flour in the bottom of a bowl with the palm of your hand. After that, you have to use two sieves, one with medium holes and the other with small holes, to separate and reduce the lumps. You then steam the grains using clear water, and dry them on a sheet in the sun while occasionally stirring them. When cooking a couscous recipe, the golden rule is to steam the grains two or three times over a meat and vegetable stew, and alternating the steaming process by sprinkling the steamed couscous with cold water and stirring the grains by hand. As for the broth, you have dozens of possibilities, but in my opinion, the most traditional recipe (recipe follows) is the best. It calls for fresh vegetables and lamb. Do not hesitate, however, to try other combinations, for example the recipes with onions and raisins, sour milk, fish, stuffed tripe or chicken with dried vegetables, sheep tripe and liver, dried beef, and the sweet *mesfoufs*, which can be delicious. I still fondly remember a *seffa*, which was cooked for me some thirty years ago by Moroccan relatives. There was butter, raisins, shelled almonds, cinnamon, sugar, and orange flower water in it. I have never had any better couscous, except perhaps for the one made by Miloud, a little Kabylian restaurant owner, and oddly enough, another, made by my friend Habib. He is Lebanese and has had the audacity to rethink the concept of the dish, while respecting the base of the Maghrebi doctrine on the matter.

I am mentioning Habib, so it will never be said again that Eastern Arabs are incapable of really appreciating couscous. I am also doing so, in order to remind my readers as often as I can, that simple things are infinitely varied. Here in France, couscous has become the archetype of the shared meal. It is in a way similar to *pot-au-feu* and *choucroute*. I was pleasantly surprised, by reading Rabelais, to learn that 16th century Provence already loved couscous. It was called "coscoton, moorish style." The woman writer George Sand wrote the first recipe in French that I was able to find dated from the 19th century C.E. She evidently loved her "kouss-kouss" quite hot with lamb or chicken, and never with beef. The second recipe is in the famous *Cordon Bleu*, which in 1895 mentioned the "Arabic couscoussou" among the "soups from abroad." We owe the third, a much more elaborate recipe, to the famous engineer Henri Babinsky, a.k.a. Ali Bab, who published his *Practical Gastronomy* in 1907. The only thing is, this author is blaming couscous for "the incredible expansion of some Arab women, front and back," which is none of his business . . .

Couscous with Lamb and Vegetables

Ksksu bel-khodra

MOROCCO

Serves 6

4½ lbs. lamb shoulder, diced
2 lbs. fine couscous grains
1 lb. carrots
1 lb. turnips
1 lb. pumpkin
1 lb. zucchini
1 lb. eggplants
1 lb. fresh fava beans
1 lb. chickpeas, soaked overnight
4 onions, sliced
2 very ripe tomatoes, peeled and seeded
2 small hot peppers (optional)
3 tbsp. olive oil
peanut oil
8 tbsp. butter
½ tsp. powdered saffron
½ tsp. ginger
½ tsp. pepper
1 bunch of parsley and cilantro, tied together
Salt

In the bottom pot of a *couscoussier** sauté the meat, spices, and sliced onions in the olive oil. Then add 3 quarts of water, season with salt, and bring to a boil. Add the chickpeas, carrots, turnips, shelled fava beans, and the tied bunch of cilantro/parsley.

Pour the couscous into a large, deep serving dish or bowl. Add in a little peanut oil and roll the couscous grains between the palms of your hands, in order to break up the clumps. Sprinkle

---

*Couscoussier *resembles a double boiler with a lid and a top pot (*keskas*) that has holes in the bottom. The stew or water is cooked in the larger bottom pot and the couscous grains are steamed on top.*

with 2 cups of water, fluff up the grains with your hand by tossing them, and then leave the grains to puff up a little before steaming them covered in the *keskas*.

Once the steam begins to rise into the *keskas*, steam the grains 15 minutes. Then pour the couscous back into the large bowl, fluff up the grains with a large spoon, and let them cool. Then sprinkle the couscous with 1 cup of cold salted water. Stir and fluff up the mixture with your hand, and then let it set until it has absorbed all of the water.

Add the tomatoes, eggplants, and squash to the pot, along with the hot peppers (optional).

Put the couscous back into the *keskas* and place it back on top of the pot. As soon as the steam rises again, steam the grains for 15 minutes. Pour the couscous back into the bowl, sprinkle with unsalted water, and fluff up the grains. Set aside.

Check the seasoning. Simmer the meat and vegetable mixture until done.

Fifteen minutes before serving, put the couscous back into the *keskas*, and place if on top of the pot until the steam starts to rise again.

Pour the couscous into the bowl, add the butter, and separate the grains by rolling them between the palms of your hands. Add the cooking juice until the couscous is saturated with it.

In a large, round, deep serving dish, shape the couscous grains into a pyramid. Remove the bunch of cilantro and parsley from the pot. Make a well in the middle of the pyramid and pour the meat and vegetables into the well.

Couscous with Dried Vegetables

Bissar

ALGERIA

Serves 4

2 lbs. fine couscous grains
1 large chicken
1 piece of qadid *(preserved beef)*
1 cup chickpeas
1 cup black-eyed peas
1 cup small dried fava beans
1 cup lentils
1 cup split peas
4 onions
1 bunch cilantro (about 1 cup)
2 tbsp. fresh basil
1 cup olive oil
1 tbsp. dried basil
1 tbsp. freshly ground coriander seeds
1 pinch hot pepper
Salt and pepper

Cut the chicken into 8 pieces and sauté with the minced onions in the bottom pot of a *couscoussier* (see note on page 103). Season with salt, pepper, basil, and ground coriander. Fill the pot ⅔ full of water and bring to a boil. Lower the heat and simmer for 30 minutes.

Meanwhile, pour the couscous grains into a large deep serving dish or bowl, add in two cups of lightly salted water, then stir and fluff up the grains. Leave them to puff up, stirring occasionally.

Add the *qadid* and dried vegetables (after soaking the chickpeas overnight, and blanching the other dried vegetables) to the meat mixture, and let it simmer another 50 minutes. Place the *keskas* on top and cover.

After the couscous has steamed for 15 minutes over the cooking stew, take the *keskas* off of the bottom pot and pour the couscous back into the large bowl. Add 1 cup of cold water, then stir and fluff it up with your hand for 10 minutes to break up the clumps. Then put the couscous back into the *keskas* and place the *keskas* back on top of the bottom pot, to steam for another 10 minutes.

Take off the *keskas* once more, then continue to stir and fluff up with your hand for 10 minutes more. Set aside.

As soon as the chicken and dried vegetables are cooked, check the seasoning and add the hot pepper, basil and cilantro. Put the *keskas* back on top of the bottom pot and let it steam for 5 minutes.

Pour the couscous grains into the bowl, add the olive oil, stir the grains around with your hand, fingers apart, and separate the clumps by rolling them between the palms of your hands.

Place the couscous in an attractive serving dish, pour on the meat and vegetables, and then the cooking juice on top.

Couscous with Sea Bream

Kusksi bil-warqa
TUNISIA

Serves 4

2 large sea breams or sea bass
2 lbs. fine couscous grains
3 tomatoes, peeled, seeded, diced
¼ cup raisins
2 quinces, cored and quartered
½ cup olive oil
½ tsp. black pepper
½ tbsp. paprika
1 pinch hot pepper
1 pinch cinnamon
1 pinch crushed rosebuds
Salt

Have the fish cleaned and cut into steaks by your butcher. Season the pieces with salt and pepper, and set aside to absorb the seasoning.

In the bottom pot of a *couscoussier* (see note on page 103), heat the olive oil and sauté the tomatoes. Season with paprika, pour in 6 cups of water, and bring to a boil, then lower the heat to simmer.

Prepare the couscous grains as explained in the preceding recipes, and steam twice in the *keskas*.

Add the raisins and quinces to the cooked tomatoes. Ten minutes later, add the fish steaks, cinnamon, and ground rosebuds. Simmer 10 minutes. Reheat the couscous grains, add the butter to the bowl used for tossing the grains, and roll the couscous grains in the palms of your hands.

Pour the grains into a large deep serving dish, make a well, and place the slices of fish in the middle, with the quinces and raisins arranged around the fish. Pour some of the cooking juice on top and serve the remaining juice in a sauceboat.

Dessert Couscous

Mesfouf or *seffa*

MAGHREB

Serves 4

2 lbs. fine couscous grains
8 tbsp. cup butter
1 cup raisins
1 tbsp. orange flower water
1 tbsp. ground cinnamon
Powdered sugar
Salt

Pour the couscous grains into a large deep serving dish or bowl. Sprinkle with 2 cups of lightly salted water. Add the raisins, then steam (as instructed in preceding recipes) toss the grains three times. Some butter must be added each time the couscous is removed from the *keskas*.

In a large deep serving dish, shape the couscous grains into a pyramid, sprinkle with orange flower water, then top with the sugar and cinnamon.

Rice

THE FRENCH DO NOT like rice very much, and I do understand their culture, though I am personally crazy about rice! What they call "rice" has generally nothing to do with the cereal that is known under that name in other countries, including my own country. Rice for them is a cereal of small white grains which may be round or long, and, they notice, every time it is served tends to be overcooked or not cooked enough when used with chicken *basquaise* or *blanquette de veau à l'ancienne*. Contrary to real rice, their "riz" has no taste, and when it does, the taste is even worse than tasteless. This is why a particular lady-friend, who loves eating, but hates bad food, says that the French only know how to use rice properly at the doors of their city halls and churches, where they throw rice by the fistful on newlyweds when wishing them wealth and fertility. I admit that this particular use is more sensible than most of their "cuisine bourgeoise" recipes, but I should not let myself go that far. There is an old belief in my country, which says: As long as there are hungry people, the person who wastes rice or wheat on the ground will have to pick it up grain by grain on Judgment Day, with his own eyelashes.

It would be wrong to conclude that rice has not inspired the good chefs in France. On the contrary, they have always been excellent in the art of baking it. Most gastronomic dictionaries, including the one written by Alexandre Dumas, mention rice in their dessert recipes. Also remember the recipes of the great chef Auguste Escoffier. Still, the Asians have made rice what it is: a civilization in itself. The Middle East is no rival to China in its quantitative rice production. Rice was born there fifty centuries ago, and was cultivated by them in the third millennium. India also claims to have been the birthplace of rice. And in Japan, rice has shaped the island's civilization. But while the Iranians, Arabs, and Turks are people of wheat; they also presented civilization with two other major contributions. The first was the introduction of rice to Africa and Europe. The second, which is much more precious, was the invention of several delicious dishes, which, because they were recommended by the Prophet, should be enough to have all of our sins forgiven.

Our cooking of rice goes back a long way. Evidently, rice began being cultivated in the Near East—more precisely in Mesopotamia—before Alexander the Great's campaigns in the East. It then spread to Northern Syria, and possibly to the Jordan valley. This means that the Arabs knew of rice, at least as a medicine, before they knew Islam. But there is no evidence that it was ever cooked in Hedjaz at the time of the Prophet. Two *hadits* do speak about it, but they are manifestly not authentic. There is also Tabari's testimony on the death of caliph Abu Bakr. The historian relates that the caliph died because he had eaten a dish of poisoned rice, but there are other testimonies to the contrary. Actually, it was only after the Arabs conquered Iraq that they became acquainted with rice. They later introduced it to areas where it had previously been unknown. Its cultivation spread over a very large area, e.g., to Syria-Palestine, and especially Egypt, but also to Southern Morocco, Sicily, and Spain. By the 10th century C.E., it had become the staple food of Eastern Africa, as confirmed by Marco Polo and later by Ibn Battouta.

One does run across a few stories of sophisticated recipes at the time of Umeyyiads, but rice remained relatively modest in gastronomy until the Abassids. By then, the production of rice around Basra in Iraq was already significant. It was served as rice-bread, and accompanied fish. Beginning in the ninth century, since both rice and fish were very cheap and abundant at the time, rice was considered to be the food of the poor. Rice bread seems to have been very popular in Iran, especially in the rice-producing provinces along the Caspian Sea and in Khuzistan, which had no less than fifty thousand ovens! The bread was made by cooking the dough on a hot plate, sprinkled with sesame or nigella seeds. Rice dishes were also numerous, and usually accompanied fish, whenever possible, or meat. In these cases, rice was cooked with milk or broth, and very often with honey, date molasses or raisins. But thanks to numerous cookbooks, we also know of many other recipes where rice was seasoned with saffron, pepper, coriander, and cooked, with or without meat, with chickpeas or lentils. In Spain, rice would be cooked in water first, then in ewe's milk—the best, according to the Spanish. A famous book from the early 13th century C.E. also has recipes with rice and sugar. It explains how to cook *harisa*, rice compote with chicken or lamb, seasoned with cinnamon.

All of these dishes have more or less disappeared, and this is too bad, for some of them would do honor to today's tables. In his very beautiful book, *La Cuisine des Califes*, David Waines tried to adapt some of the old recipes to modern day tastes, like, for example, *aruzziyya*, attributed to the legendary Abassi prince Ibrahim ibn al-Mahdi. This recipe combines smoked meat and rice, cooked in milk, which has been seasoned with ginger and cinnamon. I am sure that Ibn al-'Adim's recipes, which date back to the late 13th century C.E., could be adapted, too. We would just have to take it easy on the sugar and fat, and be quite particular about the color of the rice, using either saffron yellow, or red from Morello cherries or plums. And we couldn't forget to sprinkle the dishes with pistachios, as he suggested, being the typical Alep dweller that he was. At this time, let me mention the little treatise by Ibn al-Hadi, a Damascus polygraphist, who lived in the late 15th and early 16th century C.E. during the eve of the Ottoman conquest. It contains over a dozen rice recipes, which for the most part have disappeared, but the basic principles have not really changed. From the Ottoman period to the present day in Turkey, Syria, and Egypt, rice has always been washed, soaked and drained. It is then sautéed in butter by itself, or with meat and vegetables. Then some boiling water (or broth) is added, and it is left to simmer over low heat. The people of Iran and Iraq have another method: rice is washed thoroughly, soaked and drained, then it is cooked and drained for a second time in a pot whose bottom and sides have been well buttered. Before sealing the pot with a lid, it is covered with a cloth that absorbs the steam. There is no better rice in the world, especially if one uses the best one of all *Anbar*, but, *basmati* is quite all right too.

Take your time, my friends, when you cook rice, and you will not be disappointed. Then you will understand the meaning of a proverb, which reflects the class struggle in the kingdom of cereals: "All the prestige belongs to rice, *bulgur* be hanged." And this is why we mock a showoff by saying: "Of course, he's been eating rice!"

Saffron Rice

Tumman al-za'faran

IRAQ

Serves 4

1½ cups basmati rice
8 oz. ground lamb
1 medium sized onion, finely chopped
1½ cups chicken broth
½ tsp. saffron
½ tsp. each spice mixture (pepper, nutmeg, cinnamon, cloves)
2 tbsp. samn *(mix of butter and olive oil)*
¼ cup blanched almonds
¼ cup white raisins
2 tbsp. rose water

Carefully wash the rice several times and soak it in lukewarm water for 1 hour. In a small bowl, mix the saffron into the rose water. Set aside.

Sauté the almonds in 1 tablespoon *samn*, set them aside. Sauté the onion, add the ground lamb and spices. Mix and cook, while stirring constantly. Add the raisins to the meat mixture, season with salt. Take the pan off the heat, set aside.

Melt the remaining *samn* in a pot, add the chicken broth and 2 teaspoons of the saffron rose water. Bring to a boil. Drain the rice and add it to the pot with the chicken broth and saffron rose water. Cut a strip of cloth and place it around the rim of the pot, like a turban. Then carefully put the lid on over the strip (this technique seals the pot), and cook it over very low heat. When it is half cooked, gently mix in the ground lamb mixture.

Place the mixture in an attractive serving dish. Top with the sautéed almonds, then sprinkle with the rest of the rose water.

Rice with Fish

Sayyadiyyé

LEBANON

Serves 4

2 sea bream or bass steaks
1 lb. onions
2 cups basmati rice
½ cup flour, mixed with 1 tsp. salt and 1 tsp. cumin
1 tbsp. ground cumin
1 tbsp. ground turmeric
1 tsp. pepper
2 tsp. salt
Oil for frying

For the sauce:
3 onions
½ cup tahini *(sesame paste)*
½ cup lemon juice
¼ cup pine nuts
Salt

Wash the rice several times and drain it. Roll the pieces of fish in the flour spice mix and fry them. Set them aside to drain on paper towels. Pour some of the frying oil into a pot and sauté the chopped onions. Remove from the heat.

Place the fish at the bottom of the pot and add the rice and sautéed onions.

In another pot, bring 3 cups of water to a boil with salt, pepper, turmeric, and cumin. Slowly pour this broth into the pot over the fish, and cook, covered, over low heat, for 30 minutes. Meanwhile, sauté the pine nuts in a pan and set aside.

For the sauce, cut the onions into half-moon slices and place them in 1 cup of lightly salted cold water. Boil 15 minutes. Take off the heat and let cool. Mix the *tahini* and lemon juice together, gradually stir in the onions and broth. Pour the mixture into a sauceboat.

Arrange the rice and fish mixture in a large serving dish so that the fish pieces are on top, and sprinkle with the pine nuts.

Serve the *sayyadiyyé* with the sauce.

Rice Panada with Meat

Fatta bel-lahm

EGYPT

Serves 4

2 pita breads
1 cup round rice
2 lbs. deboned, lean lamb shoulder
1 onion
½ tsp. cardamom
½ cup. wine vinegar
2 garlic cloves, chopped
¼ cup raisins
¼ cup blanched almonds
½ tsp. hot pepper (optional)
Vegetable oil
Salt and pepper

Carefully wash the rice several times and pour it slowly into a pot with a large quantity of boiling salted water. Continue boiling 10–15 minutes, depending on the quality of the rice. Drain and rinse with cold water to keep the rice grains from sticking.

Cut the meat into approximately 15 pieces and sauté with the chopped onion. Season with salt, pepper, and cardamom. Add 4 cups of boiling water to cover, and cook until the meat is very tender.

Meanwhile, cut the bread into small squares and toast them in a pan, or broil them in the oven. Sauté the almonds separately, add the raisins, and mix the ingredients over the heat, stirring constantly, for a few minutes.

Just before serving, sauté the garlic, add the vinegar and 2 cups of hot meat broth. Let it cook a few minutes. Place half of the bread pieces in a deep serving dish, add half the rice (which has been reheated with some broth), then the pieces of meat. Season with salt, and sprinkle with the hot pepper. Cover with the rest of the rice and bread pieces, then ladle on the garlic-vinegar-broth mixture. Top with the mixture of almonds and raisins.

Rice Halva

Halawat al-ruzz

LEBANON

Serves 4

1 cup round rice
2 cups sugar
½ cup rose water
1¼ lbs. mozzarella cheese, sliced thinly

Measure 5 cups of water into a pressure cooker, add the carefully washed rice. Bring to a boil, stirring constantly with a wooden spoon, then cook under pressure for 45 minutes. Take off the heat.

Purée the rice, using a food processor, then put it back in the pressure cooker. Return the cooker to the heat, uncovered. Add the sugar and stir until it begins to boil. Cover and cook 45 more minutes under pressure.

Stir the rice and mix in the rose water. Add in the mozzarella, making sure that the mixture is perfectly homogeneous.

Pour into individual bowls, and serve hot.

Caraway Dessert

Meghli

LEBANON

Serves 8

1 cup cream of rice
2 cups sugar
6 cups water
1 tbsp. ground caraway
1 tsp. powdered cinnamon
½ tsp. powdered anise
¼ cup chopped walnuts
¼ cup shelled and peeled pistachios
¼ cup pine nuts, soaked for 1 hour
½ cup grated coconut

Carefully mix the cream of rice and spices. Pour the mixture into a pressure cooker with 2 cups of cold water. Add the sugar and 4 cups more of water, bring to a boil, stirring constantly. Cover and cook under pressure for 45 minutes

Give the mixture a stir and then simmer for another 10 minutes over low heat, stirring constantly.

Pour into individual bowls, and cover the *meghli* with coconut, then with walnuts, pistachios, and pine nuts.

Serve cold.

Bulgur wheat

THE FRENCH PRETEND TO know everything about rice. They also have a few notions about couscous, since history and geography have introduced them to it. But, they have no idea about what *bulgur* really is: a wheat that has been boiled, then dried in the sun, then ground coarsely, or "cracked." We call it *burghol*, and the Turks call it *bulgur*. Here in France, in this massively and fiercely meat-loving country, only the vegetarians know about *bulgur*. And, even they usually prefer whole rice, possibly because the Far East is more exotic than our Near East. But, this is not a reason for me to disregard it! That would be the worst possible betrayal for an Arab of the Near East! In our countries, *burghol* is both food and culture, as is couscous in Maghreb. Besides, I have meant to tell you about *kebbe* for a long time, and *bulgur* is an essential element in it. I also want to defend *tabboule*, a delicious, refreshing, and exhilarating salad, which is made with *bulgur* and parsley, and has nothing to do with the infamous thing served in France under the same name.

But let us not go too fast. Let us first attempt to find out where and how *bulgur* came about. You would think it is as old as the world, and it seems so much like part of the Near-Eastern Arab people's culture. This, by the way, is another point it has in common with couscous. And, just as when we studied its Maghreb cousin, appearances in matters of cuisine are often deceiving. I hate to disappoint my countrymen, but *bulgur* is not that old. Although it was not totally unknown to the Arabs during the classical period and already mentioned by Ibn Sayyar al-Warraq in Baghdad as early as in the 10th century C.E., it had a relatively modest place in the people's diet. No cookbook, no agricultural or dietary treatise mentioned it explicitly, and there was not one word for it in Arabic, which, by they way, is so rich and so precise. Granted, coarsely cracked wheat is called *jashish*, or *jashisha*. The lexicographer Ibn Manzur (d. 1311 C.E.) explained that our Prophet Muhammad himself is said to have cooked it for one of his wives. But, nothing indicates that this wheat was first boiled, then dried, and then cracked. The same for the three other words, which more or less mean the same thing in classical Arabic: *jarish, dashisha, burbur.* I do know the word *khadima*, which is not much in use nowadays, refers to "boiled wheat," but where is it written that this boiled wheat was then dried in the sun, and subsequently cracked? Could it be that our ancestors had no name for it because it didn't exist, and subsequently we had to borrow the word "burghul" from the Persian or Turkish languages. I would think that this happened in the 16th century C.E., for there was nothing about *bulgur* in Ibn 'Abd al-Hadi's little book, which he wrote at the beginning of that century in Damascus, but the famous physician Dawud al-Antaki, who died in 1599 C.E., did mention it. After that, one can find it mentioned more and more frequently in local chronicles and in the reports of European travelers, such as the one written by Chevalier d'Arvieux, in the mid 17th century C.E.

People tell me that the popularity of *bulgur* indicates its age. This is tantamount to saying that the potato and the tomato have been used since the beginning of time! At least in our countries, *bulgur*, as a staple, very likely dates back to the Ottoman conquest. And it seems to have spread, in general, over the lands that were once under the Ottoman Empire. I remember eating it at the tables of my Armenian, Kurdish, and Greek friends, and also, more surprisingly, in the house of Tunisian friends! I could have sworn that they were one hundred percent faithful to couscous! But, the number one place for *bulgur* is, undoubtedly, in the plains of Syria where the first ear of wheat was allegedly born. As early as the month of June, right after harvest, the wheat is boiled in huge cauldrons. It is a good opportunity for happy encounters of men and women, old and young. They sing, they dance, they chat; and love often gets its way behind the chaperons' backs. Once the wheat is cooked, it is carried up to the roofs where it is spread around to dry in the sun for several days. The children huddle around early the very next morning, waiting for a little bowl of it. It is sprinkled with sugar and nuts, a delicacy they will remember all through the year. The wheat is then cleaned and shelled before it is cracked. This is another opportunity for boys and girls in the village to get together, but this time around the millstones. Calibrating then takes place in various sieves, and this is done in order to separate the extra fine, very fine and just fine *bulgur*. What is left in the sieves is crushed into flour.

This flour, called *bsisse*, is not really worth mentioning here. The farmers use it mostly to roll dough balls or feed their chickens, and sometimes their children, with it. When feeding their children, they mix it with grape, quince or grape preserve. With the very fine *bulgur*, they make a soup, or better yet, a special bread, which is delicious when chopped onions and sour pomegranates are kneaded into the dough. But, it is the other two, the fine and large grain *bulgur*, which are most generally used. With the fine *bulgur*, people make *kebbe* dough—I'll go back to that later—whereas they cook the coarse *bulgur* as they do rice. In that case, it is cooked like pilaf, just as it is in lightly salted water, or with vegetables like tomatoes, spinach, or fava beans in a broth of lamb meat. When cooked with eggplants, it is called "the traveling Jew," or "the wandering Muslim." I have no idea why they gave it those names; perhaps they were referring to their female companions or playmates. This coarse grain mixes very well with chickpeas or lentils, like *mujaddara*, a Near Eastern dish, which was already very popular in the classical period, although it was cooked then with rice, not *bulgur*. Today, it is covered with a good amount of onions sautéed in olive oil and served with a yogurt, cucumber salad or pickled turnips. The same coarse *bulgur*, soaked in hot water and then left to ferment in curdled milk, produces *kishk*, a condiment that is very popular for its sour taste. Of the many Syrian-Lebanese-Palestinian recipes that use it, my favorite one uses *kishk* powder with lamb, which is preserved in its own fat and minced onions. People then add a few garlic cloves and some dried mint. For those who don't like lamb or garlic, you can eat it "green," just mixed with parsley, walnuts, and olive oil.

The fine *bulgur* grain is somehow destined to make *kebbe*. This is its glory and purpose. I can't say since when this began, because the history of *kebbe* is as enigmatic as the history of *bulgur*. What I can say, though, is that there has never been a better or more successful combination of meat and cereal. The two ingredients, different though they may be, blend into one, and the new element lends itself to all kinds of metamorphoses. For such osmosis, you have to start by carefully selecting the meat. It must come from a leg, or rump of a lamb. You then have to remove the nerves and fibers, and then dice the meat. If you have the courage, tell your neighbors what you are going to do, as you will have to crush the meat in a marble mortar with a wooden pestle, until it is mashed thoroughly. This will take you at least one hour. If you are lazy or in a hurry, blend the meat in an electric grinder, such as those you can see on television. The result is acceptable, though it cannot possibly be as good as meat that has been pounded by hand. Now, repeat the same operation, and this time, replace the meat with a little sheep fat, onions, salt, pepper, and mint (if you so wish). Then wash and soak the *bulgur* for a moderate amount of time, and drain it well. Add it to the paste. Knead it as long as you think fit. Crush or grind some more, occasionally adding an ice cube to the mix. Your paste is now ready, and you can eat it raw—"tartar-style." If you intend to eat it raw, halve the amount of *bulgur*. And, as in Alep, the world capital of *kebbe*, do not grind it with a mortar and pestle, season with cumin and hot pepper.

I said in a previous chapter that the people of Alep make their *kebbe* in sixty different ways. They may very well be the real inventors of this little marvel. You must know that the people around Alep produce a special *bulgur* that they are extremely proud of. It mixes in well with lamb meat, which is already excellent in the area. Some Lebanese and some inhabitants of Damascus will not hear of this, but they quickly run short of arguments. I want to remind the Syrians that they have reason to be proud of many other dishes. The Lebanese are the champions of *tabboule*, which is great, come to think of it! The French, who mistreat this salad so much, should remember this truth. The future of the French language, east of the Mediterranean, depends on it!

Tabboule

LEBANON

Serves 4

4 bunches flat parsley, chopped to equal 4 cups
1 lb. tomatoes
½ lb. fine bulgur *wheat*
½ bunch fresh mint, chopped to equal ½ cup
1 onion
Juice of 3 large lemons
½ cup olive oil
Salt and pepper
1 pinch powdered cayenne pepper (optional)

Carefully wash and drain the *bulgur*, then mix it with the lemon juice and set aside.

Finely chop the parsley, mint, and onion.

Put all of the ingredients in a large bowl. Add the olive oil, season with salt and pepper, and mix.

Serve with very tender white cabbage or romaine lettuce leaves.

Drained Yogurt with Bulgur

Kishké khadra

SYRIA

Serves 6

½ lb. labne *(yogurt)*
⅓ cup fine bulgur *wheat*
1 onion
1 bunch parsley, to equal 1 cup
¼ cup chopped walnuts
1 tbsp. ground cumin
1 tbsp. dried mint
1 tsp. hot pepper
Salt
Olive oil

Soak the *bulgur* in cold water for 5 minutes, then drain it carefully. Finely chop the parsley and onion.

In a large bowl, mix all of the ingredients and leave the mixture to set for 30 minutes in the refrigerator.

Sprinkle with olive oil and serve.

Bulgur with Tomatoes

Burghol bil-banadora

NEAR EAST

Serves 6

1 cup coarse bulgur
1 lb. tomatoes, peeled and seeded
¼ cup garbanzo beans, cooked and drained
1 onion
⅓ cup olive oil
1 tsp. cumin
1 tsp. cayenne pepper (optional)
Salt and pepper

Chop the onion and sauté it in the olive oil. Add the *bulgur* and garbanzo beans, sauté them a few minutes. Finally, add the diced tomatoes. Season with salt and pepper and the other spices, then pour in 3 cups of boiling water. Mix and simmer for 30 minutes.

Serve hot or cold.

Bulgur with Lentils

Mujaddara

NEAR EAST

Serves 4

1 cup green lentils
1 cup coarse bulgur
5 medium onions
½ cup olive oil
1 tsp. ground cumin
Salt and pepper

Sort out and wash the lentils. In the top of a double boiler, boil 3 cups of water and steam the lentils over the water. Simmer covered for 30 minutes.

Meanwhile, carefully wash and drain the *bulgur*. Add it to the lentils with the salt, pepper, and cumin, then mix and continue simmering covered until all of the liquid has been absorbed.

Meanwhile, cut the onions into half-moon slices and sauté in the olive oil until lightly colored, and remove from the pan. Pour the oil on the *mujaddara* and mix delicately. Cover and let it set a few minutes off the heat.

Place in an attractive serving dish and sprinkle with the half-moon slices of onion.

Serve hot or cold, with yogurt, lettuce, and pickles.

Bulgur Soup

Burghol jari

TUNISIA

Serves 6

1 cup bulgur
1 cup dried fava beans, shelled
½ cup olive oil
4 garlic cloves
2 tbsp. tomato paste
1 tsp. paprika
1 tsp. ground cumin
Juice of 1 lemon
Harissa *(optional)*

Wash and drain the *bulgur* and boil it in 8 cups cold water with the fava beans and the oil. One hour later, add the tomato paste, garlic clove, and paprika, and simmer for another 30 minutes.

Purée the mixture, add the cumin, lemon juice, and one teaspoon *harissa*. Mix well.

Check the seasoning and serve very hot.

Baked Kebbe

Kebbe bil-siniyyé

LEBANON

Serves 6

For the *kebbe:*
1 lb. leg of lamb, deboned
1½ cup fine bulgur
3 tbsp. samn *(mix of butter and olive oil)*
1 onion
Salt and pepper

For the stuffing:
6 oz. ground lamb
2 tbsp. samn *(mix of butter and olive oil)*
1 chopped onion
¼ cup pine nuts
Salt and pepper

First prepare the raw *kebbe:* cut the leg of lamb in large cubes and grind it, with the chopped onion, in an electric chopper. Pour the resulting paste into a large deep dish, and season it with salt and pepper. Add the *bulgur* to the meat paste. Knead vigorously so that the *bulgur* mixes perfectly with the meat.

Then prepare the stuffing by separately sautéing the onion, ground lamb, and pine nuts. Finally, mix them together and cook 2 minutes, seasoning with salt and pepper.

Place the *kebbe* (meat paste) in a bowl and chill it by placing the bowl in a larger bowl of ice water. Butter a 10 inch square baking dish and spread the bottom with half of the *kebbe*. Spread the stuffing on top of this layer. Make small patties with the remainder of the *kebbe*, and then arrange them evenly on top of the stuffing layer. Flatten them down with your hand, then cut through the layers with a knife to make 8 portions, and top with small dabs of *samn* (or butter).

Bake in a hot oven (425F°) for 40 minutes.

Serve hot with a *jajiq* salad (garlic yogurt, mint, and cucumber).

Bulgur with Lamb

Burghol bi-dfine

LEBANON, PALESTINE, SYRIA

Serves 6

2½ lbs. deboned lamb shoulder, cut into 12 pieces
3 cups coarse bulgur
1½ lbs. pearl onions
1 cup garbanzo beans, soaked overnight
1 cup samn (mix of butter and olive oil)
1 pinch of each: salt, cinnamon, ground cumin, ground caraway
¼ cup pine nuts

Sauté the meat, onions, and garbanzo beans in ½ cup of the *samn*.

Add water to cover and boil for 1 hour.

Wash the *bulgur*, drain. Sauté in a little *samn*.

Pour the *bulgur* over the meat. Add the spices.

Check the amount of the broth (it should be about 1½ times the volume of the *bulgur*), and simmer another 30 minutes over very low heat.

Sauté the pine nuts and sprinkle them on top of the dish.

Serve with yogurt.

The grape

I WANT TO TELL my dear readers right away that they will not find any consideration about wine in this chronicle. But, they should not worry: I am not abstaining from talking about it because of a sudden conversion to soft drinks! It is not hypocritical either, as are the Egyptian actresses who decide to wear a veil when they realize they are aging. On the contrary, I have too much respect for wine, and it would seem indecent for me to say only a few words, between *verjus* and fruit juice. In this sense, I am copying Abu Nuwas, one of the greatest Bacchic poets of all times, who used to tell us either to proclaim the virtues of wine, to call it by its most beautiful names, or else to keep quiet.

Having thus acquitted myself morally, I do recognize that table grapes are in a class by themselves. Since Noah planted the first vine, as soon as the Flood water had receded, it has never ceased growing and multiplying, and there are eight thousand varieties today. Not all of them are destined for the brewery, even though Noah himself and his two sidekicks, Egypt's Osiris and Greece's Dionysos, were evidently more attracted to the liquid than the solid product. I am ashamed to confess to knowing only thirty or forty of these varieties, most of them from the country of my youth. I remember the farmers giving them strange nicknames, like "mule brains," "cow's eyes," "young girls' cheeks," or "virgin girls' fingers," etc. They made us laugh or daydream. But, the most fragrant, juicy, delicate grape, named *zayni*, was so kind, that she climbed the arbors in front of our homes in the heart of the old city. I suppose that the Arab writers in the Middle Ages had *zayni* in mind when they said that the grape is the king of all fruits. Only the date was in a position to compete for this title, and the Koran combines both in many places, as evidence of Divine Goodness here and in the hereafter.

Although prohibiting Muslims from drinking wine, Islam did favor the vine. If you are not convinced of this, just read any Arabic treatise on agriculture. It will impress you with its age-old knowledge and also with our genuine closeness to the vines twirling, the sap rising, the grapes taking form. The same with botany or medicine treatises: they are all keenly interested in the various uses allotted to each part of the vine at any moment of its existence, very similar to our poetic anthologies, or our dictionaries. In the thematic dictionary written by Ibn Sidah, a genius from Andalusia who lived in the 11th century C.E., he added dozens and dozens of terms mentioning the vine, not to speak of the chapter on wine, which is even more sophisticated. As for cookbooks, I cannot pretend to have found the recipe for duck liver with grapes, but these books are full of delicious dishes. While reading them, you will see that the Arabs, from Baghdad to Cordoba, knew very well how to use green grapes. They made *verjus*, which they used to season certain salty dishes, or used it to make excellent syrup. The must from the grapes was mixed with some sun-dried fish, called *murri*, a necessary seasoning at the time. And there is Ibn Sayyar al-Warraq's book, which was published in the 10th century C.E., with more recipes for must. It is difficult to know how to react, since these books were on the border between legitimate and the fictional.

Of course, as in Rome, the lovers of the grape were hard at work, trying to find ways to keep the fruit vital beyond the fall season in order to enjoy it on the stem until spring. In the 18th Century, the great Nabulusi, a mystic from Damascus, who was also occasionally an agronomist, wrote down the methods to be used, sprinkling his text with some esoteric notes. The cunning methods dealt with the good old techniques of preservation, using salt or sugar, or better still, dehydrating the fruit, because, just like the ancient peoples of the Near East, the Arabs had been crazy about the raisin (*zabib*), and if caliph Omar apparently preferred dates, it was no doubt out of sense of loyalty to Hedjaz. As far as the physicians were concerned, the raisin was easier to digest than its prestigious competitor, and they would prescribe it for many types of illnesses. It is even said that Zuhri, one of the scribes in charge of writing down the Prophet's *hadiths*, would tell his students to eat it because it was good for their memory. *Zabib* was thus grown everywhere. The most popular variety was *kishmish*, a white seedless raisin from Khurasan. The grapes, which bunched on the stem, according to botanist Ibn al-Baytar, look like a foxtail. However, there are equally delicious varieties, like the raisin from Damascus, which has been famous in France since the 13th century C.E.; or the raisin from Alep, supposedly an aphrodisiac; or the one from Rif in Morocco, which mixes perfectly with couscous; or the one from Kabilya, which dates back to before French colonization; or the raisin from Cap Bon in Tunisia, which benefited in the 17th century C.E. from Andalusia's agricultural genius.

I will not delve too long on the culinary use of raisins, because it seems to me that they are well known. However, I must mention Morocco's thirst-quenching beverage made with raisins and seasoned with cinnamon, and the more sophisticated beverage of its kind, which is served in Lebanon under the improper name of *jullab* (from Persian *gol ab*), which means "rose water". I should also mention the jam, which an Egyptian friend had me taste, which combined raisins and cane molasses, but was not as good as jam made with fresh grapes. Still, in this chapter on desserts, my favorite is *dibs* (*raisiné*), the essential Near-Eastern concoction. It is made after a relatively long process, either from fresh grape juice, or from puréed raisins. Whenever I can get hold of it, I still love to spread it on a slice of bread with *tahini*, or, as my grandmother used to do, dip a Romaine lettuce leaf in it. This I still do, although there are more sophisticated recipes for it—like *zirbaj*, which I discovered had originally dated back to the 15th century C.E. This jam is cooked with very pleasant ingredients: pomegranate seeds, pears, jujubes, apricots, and almonds. This recipe reminds me of two delicious Alep sweets, *malban* and *jild-al-faras* ("mare skin"). Both are cooked in boiled, and reduced, grape juice, but, in the first, the pastry dough is formed around a thread and stuffed with walnuts, and in the latter, the dough is spread over a white sheet, dried and folded like a carpet.

Now as for the grape-leaves, as far as I know, they are used in two ways. One technique is to fill them with rice, with or without meat. This dish is particularly delicious (recipe follows). The other consists of wrapping small birds (the fig-pecker) in the grape-leaf and eating the whole thing in one mouthful, with the bones. This recipe is always made in the fall, when the birds have just finished stuffing themselves with figs and grapes, which gives them their very special taste. It is quite a nasty recipe. At any rate, much nastier than drinking a glass of wine . . .

Stuffed Grape Leaves

Waraq 'inab
NEAR EAST

Serves 6

80 fresh or canned grape leaves
6 lamb chops
1 lb. ground lamb shoulder
1 cup round rice
Juice of one juicy lemon
Butter
Salt and pepper

If the grape leaves are fresh; begin by boiling them for two minutes. If they are canned, rinse them well and drain them, to remove the salt.

Rinse the rice well and drain it, then mix it with the ground meat. Season with salt and pepper.

Sear the lamb chops in a little butter. Line the bottom of a pot with a few grape leaves and place the chops on top.

Spoon a little of the meat/rice stuffing into the middle of each grape leaf, fold the corners over the stuffing and then roll it up.

Place the stuffed grape leaves in the pot one by one and layer them over the lamb chops. Turn a plate upside down and lay it on top of the layers, in order to hold them in place.

Pour in enough boiling water (lightly salted) to cover the plate. Bring to a boil, and then simmer for 45 minutes. During the cooking time, add 1 cup of boiling water and the lemon juice.

Arrange the grape leaves on a serving dish, place the lamb chops on top, and serve with yogurt, to which you have added some crushed garlic and salt.

Grape Leaves with Bulgur

Wara' 'inab bil-burghol

LEBANON

Serves 4

1 lb. fresh grape leaves
1 cup coarse bulgur
2 onions
2 ripe tomatoes
Juice of 2 lemons
1 bunch parsley, to equal 1 cup
½ bunch mint, to equal ½ cup
1 cup olive oil
1 pinch paprika
Salt and pepper
2 potatoes, sliced in rounds

Rinse and drain the *bulgur* well. Dice the tomatoes and onions, then finely chop the parsley and mint. Add these ingredients to the *bulgur* and mix. Season with salt and pepper and add lemon juice and half of the olive oil, mix together.

Boil the grape leaves for a few minutes. Spoon a little of the *bulgur* stuffing into the middle of each grape leaf, fold over the corner of one leaf and then the two side leaves, then roll the leaf up rather tightly.

Line the bottom of a pot with the potato slices and place the stuffed grape leaves side-by-side and layer-by-layer on top of the potatoes. Place a plate turned upside down on top of the mixture to hold it in place. Add enough boiling water to cover the plate and pour in the remaining olive oil.

Bring to a boil, and then simmer for 30–35 minutes.

Serve cold with a side dish of yogurt mixed with crushed garlic and fresh mint.

Meat Dish with Raisins and Honey
Marqa bil-'asal
ALGERIA

Serves 6

2¼ lbs. deboned lamb shoulder
2¼ lbs. raisins
1 cup of honey
1 tsp. cinnamon
1 tsp. cubèbe*
½ tsp. saffron
½ cup butter
½ cup blanched almonds
Salt and pepper

Steam the raisins in the top of a couscous double boiler. Cool. Mix them with the honey, 1 tsp. cinnamon, and 1 pinch *cubèbe*.

Cut the meat into 6 pieces and place it in a pot. Add the butter, saffron, 1 pinch of cinnamon, 1 pinch of *cubèbe*, 1 pinch of pepper, add water to cover, and bring to a boil. Then reduce the heat, cover the pot, and simmer for 30–40 minutes. During this time, toast the almonds.

Place the meat in a deep serving dish and let it cool. Add the raisins and top with the almonds.

Serve cold.

*Cubèbe: *an aromatic pepper, supposedly from Borneo*

Refreshing Raisin Drink

Jullab

LEBANON

Serves 6

1 lb. raisiné*
8 cups water
1½ cups seeded raisins
Java incense
Pine nuts, which have been soaked in cold water

Purée the raisins. Dissolve the *raisiné* in water little by little, stirring constantly as you add water.

Light the incense burner and place it in the bottom of a pot. Cover the pot with a lid, in order to condense the incense smoke inside the pot.

Remove the lid and take out the incense burner. Then quickly pour in the diluted *raisiné* and the puréed raisins, and put the lid back on for a few minutes.

Then carefully stir the *jullab*, before pouring it into clean, dry jars.

To serve, fill glasses with cracked ice, add the *jullab*, and decorate the drink with the pine nuts and some raisins.

Raisiné: a jam made without sugar, by simmering grape juice with various fruits cut into pieces.

Raisin Jam

Ma'jun 'inab

TUNISIA

2 lbs. seeded white grapes
3 cups sugar
Juice of 1 lemon
½ cup seeded raisins
½ cup blanched almonds
½ cup hazelnuts
4 cups water

Pour the water into a large, heavy-bottomed pot. Add the sugar and lemon juice, bring to a boil, and simmer over medium heat for 30 minutes.

Add the grapes to this syrup and cook 30 more minutes. Remove the grapes and add the raisins. Continue to simmer.

Put the hazelnuts then the almonds under the broiler to brown, then drop them and the grapes into the syrup. Mix gently and simmer for 10 minutes.

The artichoke

THE ARTICHOKE IS the most mysterious of all vegetables. It is also the most feminine, as will be explained. While the male vegetables, such as the cucumber, asparagus and salsify are not afraid of exposing their arrogant virility for all to see, the artichoke, out of innate modesty (if not out of sheer flirtatiousness), goes to great lengths to hide its intimacy under petticoats and laces, folds and pleats. To get at her, her lovers must remove all her trimmings one by one. I would suggest they take their time, and go at it slowly and delicately. It's only then that the artichoke will offer her fleshiest part for them to bite into. You might want to know that, at the time when the French were less uptight, they used to call it not "bottom," but "ass." What a judicious choice of words as it is both silky and plump!

The *cynara scolymus* is feminine, but this is not the reason why the artichoke was for a long time off limits to young ladies in France. It came from Italy and crossed the Alps in the 16th century C.E. It had been totally unknown until then, and like other vegetables, the tomato for instance, it was first considered a powerful aphrodisiac. It so happened that this was just what people were looking for at the time. And the example came from on high: Queen Catherine de Médicis herself, who was not too shy on the subject, if one is to believe what Brantôme wrote about her. She was crazy about supposedly invigorating substances, such as artichoke "asses" and "cocks' combs," so much so that she almost died from overeating them at a wedding feast in 1575. But, the "exciting" career of the artichoke was not interrupted because of that. At the time of Henri IV of France, the Parisian street vendors still praised its incomparable virtues, "both for Monsieur and Madame." Much later, according to a popular poem of the

147

mid 8th century C.E., while "Madame" was frowned upon every time she ate an artichoke, she was clever enough to address herself to "Monsieur" in these terms:

> *. . . Why don't you, my beloved, eat some yourself,*
> *Since it will do me good,*
> *Better than if I were to eat it myself.*

Obviously, this charming reputation rests on nothing solid. It is, of course, by sheer coincidence that King Henry VIII, the respectable founder of the Church of England, loved women and consumed artichokes with equal appetite. Very early, in the 10th century C.E. of the Islamic world, Razes did indeed attract his readers' attention to the stimulating effects of this precious vegetable in his *Book on Food Correctives*. But, I have not read, nor heard anything anywhere that would suggest that our caliphs, sultans or kings, who had the frightening moral obligation of having to satisfy whole harems, ate it much. This is why I wonder whether Razes' *kangar* was the artichoke. And I am also not so sure about *harchaf, kharchaf, kharchouf, qinariya* . . . As for *'akkub*, mentioned by Muqaddasi, a Palestinian geographer, which my friend André Miquel translated as "artichoke," I am sure that it was the same thorny, though delicious artichoke with thistles that would draw blood from my grandmother's hands every time she insisted on cooking it for us!

Here is another mystery about the artichoke: we do not know where it came from. For many centuries, and in all of the Arabic-speaking countries, there was only one single name for all sorts of acanthus plants, thistles, and cardoons, wild or cultivated artichokes. Yet, various names were given to one plant, or one species of plant, which might very well have been the artichoke. It is close to impossible to make sense of all this. Besides, the traces were confused from the very beginning, first by the botanists themselves, from Dioscorides to Ibn al-Baytar, then by their translators, and finally by the myriad commentators who did not help to make things any easier. It seems to me that the truth is that the artichoke comes from North Africa. Our Maghreb cousins adapted a wild thistle that grew and developed. They were more interested in its ribs than in its head. This means that it was closer to the cardoon which was another vegetable derived from the thistle. The Andalusians, who were master gardeners, later tried to enlarge its head, from what we can see with Sevilla's agronomist Ibn al-'Awwam, in the 12th century C.E. From what is today Spain, the artichoke spread to Sicily, then to Naples, and finally to Florence in 1466. The Arabic word for the cardoon—*al-harchaf*, or *al-kharchaf* became *alcarchofa* in Spanish, then *articcioco* in Lombardian, then *artichaut* in French. During the 19th century C.E., the Near Eastern Arabs discovered what it had become after such a long time, and they called it *ardichoki*—a remarkable name indeed—since it was putting the final touch to the cycle of all these borrowed names, while keeping its origin as a thistle.

No wonder Maghreb is still today, in Italy, the number one place for the artichoke and the cardoon. Unfortunately, the French have ignored cardoons for too long—against Grimod de la Reynière's own prudent advice. He considered the artichoke as the *"nec plus ultra* of human science." He alleged that "a chef who is capable of cooking an exquisite dish of cardoons may be called the best artist in Europe." Unfortunately, there are very few such chefs in Europe any longer, if they exist at all! But, there are plenty of them in Morocco where the cardoon *qanariya* is so delicate that it is used in a *tadgine* to test the quality of the new olive oil. There is another *tadgine* with wild artichoke bottoms. Fava beans, or green peas, may be added to it. It is one of the most delicate dishes ever to be eaten on this planet. Still, you need a lot of courage and self-dedication to cook it, for this particular artichoke looks like a crown of thorns, but Heaven awaits you at the end of this ordeal. If you are not ready to sacrifice yourself for your guests, but still want them to be pleased, don't hesitate to try the *tadgine* with cultivated artichokes, or Tunisia's *gannariyya*, an artichoke stew with lemon and hot pepper, or Algeria's *qarnoun*, artichoke bottoms stuffed with ground meat, onions, and parsley. The stuffing is mixed with one egg and seasoned with black pepper and some cinnamon. I saw my neighbor from Constantine place them in a baking dish, add meatballs made of the same stuffing, and then bake them in a tomato sauce. Her recipe is different from ours but it is every bit as good.

Don't think, though, that my singing the praises of Maghreb's artichokes shows my lack of consideration for the French ones. On the contrary, I know of no better, except perhaps for Italy's *poivrades*, which are eaten simply, with a few grains of salt. So, if you live in the country of the Loire Valley, and crave artichokes and artichoke hearts, don't be shy: Cook and eat the many varieties, the small purple artichokes from the Midi, the *camus* from Brittany, or the large green ones from Laon, and try the many recipes available. The artichoke is always tasty, it is fun, is rich in vitamins and low on calories. It helps you to digest and pass water. It is good for many other things. And, if it is not really an aphrodisiac, it can become one, if you just believe it!

Artichokes in Olive Oil

Ardi-chokî bil-zeit

LEBANON

Serves 4

8 medium-sized artichokes
1 cup pearl onions
1 lb. fresh fava beans
Juice of 1 lemon
1 tsp. flour
½ tsp. white pepper
¾ cup olive oil
Salt

Remove the leaves and the center of the artichokes and place the bottoms in water with lemon juice. Shell and peel off the outer layer of the fava beans. Peel the onions.

Pour the oil into a pot and sauté the onions until lightly colored. Add the flour and mix it in with the onions. Then add the artichoke bottoms and fava beans. Season with salt, add water to cover, and bring to a boil.

Lower the heat and simmer for 30 minutes. Arrange the artichoke bottoms on a serving dish and fill them with the fava bean/onion mixture. Top with the sauce and cool.

Serve cold with other starters.

Artichoke Fritters

Mbattan gamnariyya

TUNISIA

Serves 4

½ lb. deboned, ground leg of lamb
12 artichoke hearts
Juice of ½ lemon
2 minced onions
2 eggs
½ cup grated cheese
1 cup minced parsley
4 tbsp. flour
½ tsp. paprika
Olive oil
2 tbsp. tomato paste
Harissa
Salt and pepper

Cook the artichoke hearts in lightly salted water with the lemon juice, then purée them. Mix the purée with the meat, parsley, onion, grated cheese, salt, and spices.

Make small meat balls, and roll them in the beaten eggs, then in the flour. Fry them in the olive oil.

Dilute the tomato paste and *harissa* together in a cup of water, add a little olive oil, and bring this mixture to a boil. Check the seasoning, then reduce the tomato sauce over low heat.

Serve hot with the sauce on the side.

Stuffed Artichokes

Ardi-choki mahchi

SYRIA

Serves 4

8 artichoke bottoms rubbed with lemon juice
¾ lb. ground lamb shoulder
2 chopped onions
¼ cup pine nuts
Olive oil or samn *(mix of butter and olive oil)*
Salt, pepper, cinnamon

Fry the artichoke hearts in the oil or *samn*, and set them aside on a plate.

In the same frying pan, sauté the ground meat and onions, then the pine nuts. Season with salt and pepper.

Fill the artichoke bottoms with the meat mixture and place them in a baking dish. Add hot water to cover and bake 45 minutes in a moderate oven.

Serve with rice pilaf.

Artichoke Stew

Mderbel qarnoun

ALGERIA

Serves 6

2 lbs. deboned lamb shoulder
12 artichoke hearts
4 cloves garlic
Juice of 1 lemon
2 tbsp. samn *(mix of butter and olive oil)*
½ cup garbanzo beans (soaked overnight)
½ tsp. cinnamon
½ tsp. caraway seeds
1 tbsp. vinegar
Salt and pepper
1 sprig of fresh basil

Cut the artichoke hearts in medium-sized slices and rub them with lemon juice. Fry them in a pot, then take them out and set them aside, keeping them warm.

Cut the meat in 6 pieces and place it in the pot. Sear it on all sides. Add the garbanzos, crushed garlic cloves, spices, and a little salt. Add water to cover and simmer for 40 minutes.

Add the artichoke slices to the pot and simmer another 15 minutes.

Just before serving, add the vinegar and chopped basil and bring the mixture to a boil.

Tadgine of Artichokes and Fava Beans

Tâjin bel-qouq wel-foul

MOROCCO

Serves 6

2 lbs. lamb shoulder, cut in 8 pieces
4 tbsp. olive oil
1 clove garlic, crushed
1 tsp. ginger
1 pinch saffron
8 artichoke bottoms rubbed with lemon juice
1½ cup shelled fresh green fava beans
1 preserved lemon (rind only)
A few green olives
salt

Place the meat in a pot and add the oil, garlic, ginger, saffron and salt. Add water to cover and simmer over medium heat, adding water from time to time.

Put the beans in a saucepan and cook them in half of the meat sauce. Add water. Do the same process with the artichokes in another pan.

Add the bean and the artichoke mixtures to the meat mixture and put in the thinly sliced preserved lemon rind, along with the green olives. Bring the mixture to a boil.

Arrange the meat in a deep serving dish and cover the meat with the fava beans and artichoke bottoms. Next add the olives and top with the sauce.

Note: Fresh peas can be substituted for the fava beans.

Shakshuka with Artichokes and Fava Beans

Shakchoukit gannariyya w foul

TUNISIA

Serves 4

4 artichokes
1 lb. fresh fava beans
2 onions
2 carrots
½ lb. merguez *sausages (spicy lamb or beef sausage)*
2 pinches of ground coriander seeds
2 pinches of ground caraway seeds
4 eggs
½ cup olive oil
2 cloves garlic
Juice of ½ lemon
Salt and pepper

Remove the leaves and centers of the artichokes and cut the hearts in quarters. Place them in a bowl of water with the lemon juice. Shell and remove the outer layer of the fava beans. Peel the carrots and cut them in rounds. Crush the garlic with a little salt.

In a high sided frying pan, heat the oil over medium heat and sauté all of the vegetables together with the *merguez*, cut in ½ inch slices. Add salt, pepper, caraway, and coriander. Pour in 1 cup of water and cover with a lid. Simmer 10 minutes over medium heat, then 20 minutes over low heat.

Check the seasoning, then break the 4 eggs into the mixture and simmer a few minutes covered with the lid.

Serve immediately.

The apple

ALTHOUGH THIS CHRONICLE is dedicated to the apple, I do not feel duty-bound to give you another rendering of Adam and Eve's adventure. Besides, you will not see in the Bible if the forbidden fruit was an apple, a fig or an apricot, and this is a good thing for all of us, in particular for the street vendors. Whatever the fruit of the Tree of Knowledge of Good and Evil may have been, we do have to admit that the moral of the story is very immoral. As Diderot once said, what we learn is that God prefers His apples to His children! I tend to prefer the legend of the golden fruit in the Garden of Hesperides (it is more positive, since it presents the apple tree as the Tree of Life) or the curious tale of the Apple of Discord, without which Paris would never have abducted the beautiful Helen of Troy, and Homer would have never written the *Iliad*.

But, rather than dwell on the myths, which everyone knows by heart, I invite those who truly love the apple to discover its secret themselves. To do so let them pick one, any kind, and cut it in two, widthwise. They will discover a five-pointed star, the symbol of knowledge and power, in the middle of each apple half. With some imagination, they will be able to recognize these themes, which have been developed in most of the stories about the apple since the beginning of time. Afterwards, let them cut another apple, lengthwise this time, between the stem and what looks like a bellybutton, a perfectly normal person cannot help but see in this the image of the female sexual organ. This now will evoke other kinds of stories for them, where the apple represents earthly desires, a marvelous food and everlasting renewal. Instead of looking at the fruit, let them touch it gently feeling its roundedness, its curves, and supple soft skin, and they will understand the essence of exquisite femininity.

So, if you have ever wondered why the emperor in Byzantium was holding in his hand an apple with a cross on top, an artificial apple to be sure, but an apple nevertheless, you now know why: the emperor was telling his subjects that he dominated the whole world with his power. Venus had an apple too. The message was obviously different, not as preposterous and rather friendlier: she was aiming to become for all times the symbol of terrestrial love. I can prove that our ancestors the Arabs, those lovers of love in all its forms, although not ignorant of the first meaning, gave more importance to the second meaning of the apple. I will get back to this later. In the meantime, let me emphasize one major historical fact: almost all of the peoples from the Old World, and we are no exception, have known and joined in the praise of the apple in its wild and cultivated forms. The Egyptians passionately loved the apple: Ramses II had apple trees planted along the Nile river. King Solomon in the Song of Solomon idealized the apple. It was a favorite of the Greeks, then the Romans, and eventually rooted itself in many countries along the Western part of the Mediterranean as the fruit of all fruits. It was given the generic name for all fruits, *pomum*, and lent its own name to other less frequently eaten fruits, like the apricot, also known as the "Armenian apple," or the peach, called the "Persian apple," and even, a few centuries later, to the tomato, which was called the "golden apple," or the "love apple."

It is rather strange to see the praise of the medicinal qualities of the apple by Ibn al-Baytar, in the 13th century C.E., in his *Treatise of the Simples*. Indeed, though it was very popular in Islamic countries, the apple was not as universal as the fig or the date. The great botanist was probably displaying his loyalty to the ancients, if not to apples. Before him, in 8th century C.E. Baghdad, Hunayn ibn Ishaq, a physician and an excellent translator, was also infatuated with apples. He preferred the Syrian varieties, the *fathi* in particular, which the connoisseurs appreciated for their fragrance. He had one every day, and a quince as well, after drinking quite a bit of aged wine. Thirty thousand apples of this variety were shipped every year to the palace of the caliph. The *fathi* was also very popular in Cairo during the times of the Ayyubids and the Mameluks. The Copts would offer the apple to their priests for Epiphany, as did the ancient Egyptians before them. And it was only one of the many varieties that could be bought in Damascus, according to the vivid report of Badri, an Egyptian traveler who was always looking out for savory discoveries. I would also like to talk about the Lebanese apples. The poets Abu Nuwas and Mutanabbi, and those from faraway Spain, celebrated by another poet, Ibn Khafaja, mentioned them in the same terms. I presume that there were plenty of these apples in Maghreb too, which tasted and smelled heavenly, in contrast to today's apples' paltry fragrances! In any case, I know for certain that there was an apple in Djerba, Tunisia, which was rumored to "cheer up sad people's hearts." It must have been the same kind of apple as the one the beloved mentions in the *Song of Solomon*: "Bring me back to life with apples, for I am sick, sick with love."

Let us get to the point: No other fruit lends itself better to the love metaphor than the apple. In Arab poetry, everything, including the apple's shape, taste, aroma, color, and consistency, is used to celebrate the female body. It describes the cheek, mouth, breast, and hip. It is sometimes the symbol of all the senses, a concentrated pleasure, as in a famous poem by Kairouan's poet Ibn Rashiq (d. 1071 C.E.). In it, the apple represents the plump female bottom, where he can touch, smell, and taste the fruity flavor of her lips, and see the glow of her cheeks. In order to express such feelings, the Arabs, like the Greeks, used to throw to their loved ones, whether a woman or a man, an apple that had already been bitten! Ibn al-Mu'tazz, a caliph for one day, put it nicely in a poem: "a bitten apple is a messenger of kisses." Many later poets further developed this concept. Of course, this behavior is not practiced anymore, but let us remember what the Syrian poet Badawi al-Jabal once whispered to Ma'arri, a genius, but a woman hater: "If you only had known the pleasure of the apple!" Another Syrian, Niza Qabbani, alluded to Lesbian pleasures by evoking two apples brushing against each other. This much said, the apple also bore the symbolism of wisdom and power in the classical age, as can be seen in the traditional science of dreams.

The Omeyyad caliph Hisham ibn 'Abd al-Malik once dreamed about a very small quantity of apples, and subsequently quit eating them. Fortunately, his subjects were wiser: not only did they eat their fresh apples, but were also sensible enough to use them for cooking. As early as in the 10th century C.E., Baghdad's Ibn Sayyar al-Warraq offered a recipe for a *khabis* cooked with Lebanese apples. They had been peeled, seeded, dried, and then ground. The powder was mixed with a little flour, then placed in a pot with some melted butter. Honey was then added, some almond oil, a few pistachios, and some rosewater. The mixture was stirred constantly as it cooked. Once done, it was allowed to chill, then sprinkled with sugar. I found another savory recipe in Baghdadi's treatise, which dates back to the 13th century C.E., and several others in a cookbook by Ibn al'Adim, who was from Alep and lived at approximately the same time. Within the cookbook, there was a rich *zirbaj* with at least eleven ingredients (meat, chickpeas, vinegar, honey, saffron, quinces, apples, almonds, jujubes, pistachios, fresh mint), and another stew with sour apples and Swiss chard stalks. During that period, as in modern-day Morocco, a few lamb (or chicken) dishes were cooked in Spain with firm and sour apples, or with quinces. Later, at the turn of the 15th century C.E., according to the famous polygraphist Ibn 'Abd al-Hadi, people were also cooking with apples in Damascus. But, cider is never mentioned in any of these books. This is particularly astonishing on the part of Ibn Sayyar, for he never hesitated to mention fermented beverages. Cider did exist though, not in Lebanon or in Syria as would be expected, but in Iraq, if we believe a bacchic poet who knew what he was talking about.

What else can I say, except that the apple is one of the healthi-est foods, as perhaps it contains more vitamins than all the other fruits? Besides its many benefits, which all of us have been told about since we were children, Razes added the idea of the apple's alleged properties for generating forgetfulness. This is more than a good reason, in this horrible end of the century, for us to eat one everyday!

Tuffâhiyya
(Medieval Arabic recipe)

Serves 4

1 lb. lamb shoulder, cut in 8 pieces (or a medium-sized chicken)
2 large tart apples
1 onion cut in half-moon slices
¼ cup blanched almonds
Olive oil
Salt, pepper, ground coriander seeds, dried mint powder
1 cinnamon stick and ground cinnamon
Ground ginger

In a pot, sear the meat in a little oil. Add the onion, then a pinch of coriander and salt.

Once the meat is seared, cover it with hot water and add the ginger, mint, and pepper, as well as the cinnamon stick. Simmer over very low heat for 30 minutes.

Remove the cinnamon stick and cut the apple in quarters. Put the apple pieces and the almonds into the pot. Sprinkle the mixture with the ground cinnamon and place it back on the heat, simmer about 20 minutes.

Note: Recipe idea borrowed from David Waines, La Cuisine des Califes. *According to the original recipe, which is found in the book of Baghdâdî, the meat is cooked in apple juice.*

Mutton and Apples

Ghalmi b-teffah

ALGERIA

Serves 4

1 lb. lamb shoulder, cut in 8 pieces
2 pounds tart apples
1 onion, quartered
¼ cup blanched almonds
Salt, pepper, sugar, butter or samn *(mix of butter and olive oil)*
Saffron, ground cinnamon
Orange flower water
Juice of ½ lemon

Sauté the meat and the onion over low heat, and when they are brown, add water to cover. Add a pinch of cinnamon, saffron powder, and a small amount of salt and pepper.

While the meat continues to cook slowly, peel the apples, then cut them in quarters and core them. Rub them with the lemon, add to the meat 20 minutes before serving, along with a teaspoon of sugar and orange flower water. Meanwhile, brown the almonds in the *samn*.

To serve, discard the onion quarters and arrange the meat in a round serving dish, surrounded by the apple pieces. Top with the almonds and a pinch of cinnamon.

Note: You can make a richer version of this dish by adding prunes, in which case you should leave out the sugar.

The chickpea

I N S P I T E O F its undeniable merits, the chickpea has never had the honor of literary praise, nor been accepted in mythology. Could it be because of its modest origin? This is not like the fava bean, to which it is related, which has had a brilliant career in semiology—the realm of signs. To this day, the fava bean represents either the first product of the earth, or the gift of the dead to the living, or the embryo, as can be seen every year in France's *galette des rois* (Kings' cake) on the day of the Epiphany. Is it because the chickpea has not been especially blessed by nature? How ugly it is with its hairy pod and rolled up horn, which earned it the nickname of "ram's head"! As far as I know, lentils are not very good-looking either, yet, according to the Book of Genesis, Esau, on returning from the fields after a hard day's work, yielded his birthright to Jacob in order to eat them. Alas! There is nothing of the sort with the chickpea. The only historical mention is that it derived its Latin name, *cicer*, from the Cicero family. But, we do not know whether the name comes from the fact that they were chickpea merchants, or because of the famous orator who had an ugly mole on his nose, in the shape of a *cicer*. Some of us may also know of Charlemagne's famous capitulary in the year 812 C.E. The King of the Franks ordered in this book that beans be grown in his imperial gardens. But there is no precise indication as to whether these beans were chickpeas or what they were to be used for.

In any case, in spite of the special concern on the part of the King, I must recognize that in France, the chickpea has been the least important of all dried legumes—a freak, so to speak, a pariah, and a despised resident alien. This low status becomes even more bizarre when we learn how the physicians and botanists of Antiquity all believed that it had extraordinary powers. In the 15th century C.E., the Egyptian polygraphist, Suyouti, in his *Medicine of the Prophet*, summed chickpeas up in one sentence which was evidently inspired by the ancients: He said, "the chickpea is to the body what yeast is to dough." The chickpea raises our organism in every sense of the word, and as Oribases wrote earlier, "it passes on to us three of its own properties: heat, which excites our sexual desires; humidity, which increases our seeds; and wind, which swells up our veins." I guess this is why the Greeks, and later the Arabs, gave it to their stallions as fodder. Perhaps this explains Charlemagne's taste for peas, whatever the variety was, and his passion for young women, which is evidenced by his four weddings and the impressive number of his concubines. Stendhal, a fine observer of love, evidently did not know about this when he wrote in his diary on March 25, 1808, "Sovereign medicine against love: peas." I personally see in such a harsh judgment the harmful influence of the chefs in Stendhal's time. They were the sworn enemies of dry beans and peas, as can be seen in their cookbooks. There is just no mention of the chickpea in the *Dictionnaire portatif de cuisine*. The reason was probably that the chickpea is the cause of "thundering digestions," as Flaubert wrote in *La Tentation de Saint Antoine*. Sheikh Nafzawi was assuredly wiser when he advised his flagging contemporaries to drink a potion made up of chickpeas, onions and honey.

I will not dwell too long on the issue, pleasant as it is, for I believe that men and women do not live only from aphrodisiacs. Once in a while, they do dedicate themselves to certain activities, cooking for one, and they do not have to focus on sex all the time. This is why I would like to urge them not to forget the chickpea. It can give them healthy satisfactions, provided they know how to use it, of course!

So, what is one to do? First, one should start by avoiding canned peas, though Odile Godard in her *Soupers de Schéhérazade* tolerates, and even recommends them. What bothers me most, to be truthful, is that Godard suggests canned chickpeas for *hummus*, which is exactly where I would strongly advise against them. Has she decided to push cruel Shahriyar to have Scheherazade executed, and interrupt the *One Thousand and One Nights*? On the contrary, chickpeas must be soaked for at least twelve hours in lukewarm water, but whether it is necessary to add any baking soda is debatable. Some deem it indispensable, others do not, and I agree with them. It is actually necessary, even indispensable, when one wishes to soften chickpeas for a purée or a soup to use baking soda, but then only while the chickpeas are cooking. Still, you should know that not everybody agrees. Some discard the water in which the chickpeas have soaked, sauté the chickpeas by themselves in a pan for about five minutes, then sprinkle them with a teaspoon of baking soda, and finally pour some boiling water over them. Others think that once the water has been discarded, it is enough to mix the soaked chickpeas with the baking soda, and cook them in water, preferably boiling. Another serious issue is whether the chickpeas should be peeled, and, if so, when? I will not elaborate on this process as it would take too long, and because it depends on what you want to do. If you want to cook *hummus*, don't bother as the baking soda has taken care of the problem. If you need to cook with whole chickpeas, e.g., if they must be soft and solid, I strongly advise that you spread the pre-soaked peas over a level surface, go over them with a rolling pin, then put them back into some lukewarm water, and you will be astonished at how easily they will shed their skins, and leave their undesired coats floating in the water.

You might tell me: all this is well and good, but what are we to do with those chickpeas that are neither destined for a purée, a salad, or ingredients in a couscous? This is a good question, and so I eventually decided to write the great *Treatise on the Chickpea* with my friend Robert Bistolfi, which we believe has been hitherto missing in gastronomic literature. Our treatise offers dozens of recipes, which we collected from all over the world, and tested with much love. For a start, you should try the Damascus *panade*. It is definitely country cooking, but it is extremely tasty! Other simple recipes are *lablali*, a Tunisian soup with olive oil and cumin that is very popular in poorer households, or the Lebanese *makhluta*, and Egyptian *kushari*, which uses different legumes and cereals. There is *falafel*, from the Near East. Contrary to *ta'miyya*, which is made in the Nile Valley, it mixes chickpeas and fava beans. One step higher is *harira*, which is cooked by our Maghreb brothers, in particular in Morocco. It is actually so superior in taste, that I can quietly assert there is no better soup in the whole world.

A very large number of *q'dra* recipes come from Morocco. I am speaking of the many tagines with *samn* (a mixture of butter and olive oil), where the chickpeas are mixed with almonds, or with rice or potatoes, or better still, turnips. They remind us that our humble legume is not necessarily a poor relative living on a few handouts. The Arab chefs in the Classical Age understood this. I am thinking of a magnificent dish, which was allegedly created by Prince Ibrahim ibn al-Mahdi. It was given a pretty name: *'achiqa* (lover). It basically calls for chickpeas, spinach, chicken (or duck), ground lamb, almonds, walnuts, and pistachios. It was seasoned with cilantro and *verjus*.

I now would like to mention *ghraybe*, popular pastries made with chickpea flour, and the candy in which the toasted chickpeas replace the almonds, or the sesame seeds. Toasted chickpeas, *qdame* (from the classical Arabic *qudama*) are salted, sprinkled with hot pepper, or sugar, or served alone. They have been offered for centuries as starters all around the Mediterranean Sea. The Romans would swallow them with relish in the arenas, watching the Christians being devoured by lions. We are still doing the same in front of our TV sets, and what we see is not much nicer.

Chickpea Panade

Fattet hummus

SYRIA

Serves 6

1½ cups chickpeas
½ cup tahini (sesame paste)
Juice of 2 lemons
2 pieces of stale bread
3 cloves garlic
1 tsp. baking soda
2 tbsp. pine nuts
Samn (mix of butter and olive oil) or butter
Salt, pepper, ground cayenne pepper powder, finely chopped parsley

Soak the chickpeas overnight, then cook them in 8 cups of water with the baking soda. Cool. Purée half of them, then mix in the *tahini*, lemon juice and crushed garlic with a little salt. The *hummus* shouldn't be too thick.

Make bread crumbs out of the bread slices. Spread the breadcrumbs in a soup terrine with the other half of the chickpeas.

Cover this mixture with the *hummus* (puréed chickpea mixture) and top with minced parsley, the pepper and the hot pepper.

Brown the pine nuts in the *samn*, and sprinkle the mixture on top.

Note: A mixture of yogurt and crushed garlic, topped with pomegranate seeds, can replace the hummus layer.

Tadgine of Mutton Shanks

Tajine hergma

MOROCCO

Serves 6 to 8

6 to 8 mutton shanks, cut into three pieces
1½ cups chickpeas
1 cup bulgur
2 onions
1 cup olive oil
1 level tsp. paprika
1 level tsp. powdered ginger
1 pinch cayenne pepper

Soak the chickpeas overnight. The next day, remove the outer peel of the beans.

Rinse the *bulgur* before crushing it with a mortar and pestle.

Put all of the ingredients into a cast iron enamel pot (or preferably into a *tadgine* pot, if available)—the chickpeas, cracked or *bulgur* wheat, the mutton shanks, the minced onions, spices, and olive oil.

Mix everything together, add a little salt, then pour in water to cover.

Simmer, covered, for a long time. Add water if the liquid tends to evaporate. Check the seasoning before serving.

The pistachio

WHERE DOES THE PISTACHIO come from? "From Iran, of course, like the walnut and the pomegranate," my Iranian friends will say immediately. And, though they are not wrong, they are not quite right, either. The pistachio does owe a lot to their marvelous country, starting with its name, *pesteh*, which became *pistàkia* in Greek, *pistacia* in Latin, and *fustuq* in Arabic. But, to another country, Syria, it owes something, which is perhaps even more important—its fame. Remember the story of Joseph, at the end of the Book of Genesis: Jacob himself advertised for the pistachio, mentioning it as one of the best products of Canaan, along with the almond and *misk* (gum Arabic). The Romans got acquainted with it in Syria. Pliny the Elder wrote that Rome's refined governor, Lucius Vitellus, not to be mistaken for his son Aulus, the gluttonous emperor, introduced Rome to the pistachio in the year 37 C.E. About the same time, a Greek physician and botanist, Dioscorides, said that Syria's pistachios were the finest of all, and another Greek physician, Galen, confirmed his appreciation one century later. The two scholars had no way of guessing that their respective countries, Turkey and Greece, were, today, going to become the home for pistachio trees in the 20th century C.E. The pistachios which are harvested there are quite tasty. And, although they are less fleshy than those from Iran or Syria, they are sometimes even better. Besides, their size, consistency, color and taste, they are identical, so their similarities save them from the constant bickering that has gone on between the Greeks and the Turks for so long . . .

Let us concentrate on Syria. And, when I say "Syria," I of course mean Alep, and its surrounding area. In one of its orchards east of the prestigious city, I had, as a child, the incredible opportunity of admiring the pistachio growing in bunches on those magical drupes that open up at night and crackle in their red robes when the moon is full. It has always been quite rare in the whole Arab East to utter the word *fustuq* without the adjective *halabi*, "from Alep." It is a way of ascertaining both the origin and quality of the *fustuq*, just like *Apellation d'Origine Contrôlé* labels a French wine. But, the real connoisseurs are not content with these general considerations; they will go further, and distinguish between the *'ashuri* (the finest), the *baturi* (the earliest) and two other varieties, the rather banal *'ajami*, and the *jahhashi* the "donkey," whose nickname supposedly comes from the fact that its hull is so hard that only a donkey can crack it open. Don't get mixed up because of their animal-inspired names; the *jahhashi* are not the *nab-al-jamal* "camel's fangs." This is quite another variety and they are named for their long and pointed shapes. Besides, they are not the only Alep pistachios with an animal-inspired name! You can also chew into *lisan al-'usfur*, or "bird tongues," which are very small but quite delicious. I imagine that these pistachios earned their pretty name because of their slit-opened hulls, somewhat like the toasted and salted pistachios, which the poet Ibn Sukkara described in the 10th century C.E. He compared their half open hulls to the bills of a bird, and the edible insides to their tongues. The image is rather pleasant, it reminds me of another much older simile, which was developed over the centuries by a good dozen landscape poets, from Ibn al-Mu'tazz to Sanawbari. In their prose, the pistachio was likened to an emerald in a silk veil, nested in an ivory jewel, and set in a ruby gem because of its triple protective coverings.

Of course you know that I am not quoting this prose because of its debatable poetic value! The evocation of these precious stones carries us away towards a world of luxury and voluptuousness, and this is what I am getting at: the pistachio is to be found in the richest fillings, the finest candy, and the most exquisite desserts. They sometimes come dangerously close to being scandalous. *Maqrizi*, in his *Khitat*, reported that a Fatimid cadi would offer his guests musk dragées (candied coated nuts), but most of them were pistachio nuts, and a few were little balls of gold . . . Since his feasts often ended in a free-for-all, the perverse judge eventually had to give up his little game. Fortunately, Arab literature mentions other uses for the pistachio. While still luxurious, they will not excite men's greediness, but sharpen their appetites. I am thinking of *tayafir*, Cairo's specialty, mentioned by Maqizri himself, or of *natif*, which the geographer Ibn Hawqal tasted in Manbij, not far from Alep. It was prepared with raisins, nuts, pistachios and sesame seeds. Alep's historian Ibn al-'Adim deliberately introduced pistachios in a good many savory, sweet, or sweet and savory recipes. Most of the time, they are toasted, then ground or puréed. Among these recipes, I especially like the stews in which the pistachio is combined with an acid fruit, like the quince or the apple, or with sweet vegetables, like the squash or the carrot. And I tend to believe that it is no surprise that the chefs in Paradise, according to Ma'arri in his *Epistle on Forgiveness*, have been selected from Alep, generation after generation!

This said, you should know that the Europeans, in particular the French, have no reason to blush at what they have done with the pistachio, or rather, at what their ancestors did with it. I am not alluding here to the pig's head or the *mortadella*, or the wrongly called "pistachio ice creams," but to the astonishing recipes which Jean de la Lune created in 1656 C.E.: pies with pistachio, cinnamon, amber and musk; green "nulle"[1] with pistachio, Swiss chard juice and pomegranate seeds; pistachio omelets, soups, donuts, and pastas. And a mysterious L.S.R. added in 1674 C.E.: a pistachio jam, several small and large pistachio cakes, and a pistachio cream, flavored with orange flower water and lemon rind. The 18th century C.E. went even further. I am thinking of the pistachio diablotins, meringues and dragées in the famous *Dictionnaire portatif de cuisine*. These delicious dishes are today no more than a vague memory, but we can find them here and there on very special tables, as eaten by the beautiful Haydée and Don Juan, in Lord Byron's famous poem. The pistachio lovers

[1] A kind of custard made with egg yolk, sugar and cream

must look to the East to fulfill all their desires with at least two Alep marvels, *karabidj* and *kunafa ballouriyya*, and two Damascus delicacies—a *baklava*, named *kul wa-shkur* (literally "eat and thank the Lord"), and *kunafa mabruma*. But, they will not be disappointed with other Alep specialties, such as *siwar al-sitt* (the "lady's bracelet"), *ghazl al-banat* (the "young girls' spinning"), *buqjat al-'arus* (the "bride's bundle"), and the incomparable *mamouniyya*, sprinkled with pistachios and served with crème fraîche.

There is a final delicacy, which is comparable to no other. A Damascus candy maker created it in a moment of inspiration. First, you have to have apricots from the Ghouta gardens in Damascus. They are picked ripe, then preserved according to the rules. These fragrant, beautiful apricots will melt in your mouth. You then toast and lightly caramelize some Alep pistachios, and stuff the apricots with the pistachios. If you are offered this delicacy someday, do not grab too many pieces, choose no more than one or two of the apricots, and take your sweet time savoring them, concentrating on the deep meaning of what you are doing. Then you will know Syria's subtle taste.

Chicken with Raisins and Pistachios

Mrayche

TUNISIA

Serves 4

1 chicken
½ cup raisins
1 cup shelled pistachios
1½ cups olive oil
2 cups milk
1 lb. fine semolina
Salt and pepper

Mix the semolina with half of the olive oil, a pinch of salt, and a little warm water. Knead the dough carefully and leave it to set. Then roll it out into thin tortillas and cook them in a frying pan.

Cut the chicken in 8 pieces and fry it in ⅓ cup olive oil. Season with salt and pepper, add water to cover, and simmer for 20 minutes.

While the chicken is cooking, soak the raisins in a little warm water and toast the pistachios a few minutes in the oven or in a frying pan, with no oil. Drain the raisins.

Break the tortillas into bite size pieces and put them into a large bowl. Add the scalded milk and the chicken broth, arrange the chicken pieces on top, and sprinkle with the raisins and pistachios.

Almond Milk Dessert

Kichk al-fuqara'

NEAR EAST

Serves 6

8 cups milk, scalded
½ cup cream of rice
1¼ cup sugar
2 cups blanched almonds
¾ cup chopped pistachios
2 tbsp. rose water
2 tbsp. orange flower water

Crush the almonds with a mortar and pestle. Put them in a cheesecloth bag and add a little water or, preferably, milk, and crush them. Squeeze the juice of the almonds into a bowl, then crush the almonds again, and repeat this process until all the juice of the almonds has been extracted.

Dissolve the cream of rice into the almond juice, which you have saved, add the orange flower water, rose water, and pour the mixture into a saucepan with the scalded milk. Bring to a boil and gradually add in the sugar, simmer for an hour over medium heat, stirring constantly.

Your dessert is ready when it sticks to the spoon. Pour it into bowls and let it cool. Sprinkle generously with pistachios and serve.

Pistachio Halva

Halawat al-fustuq
NEAR EAST

Serves 12

1 lb. shelled pistachios
2 cups sugar
Juice of ½ lemon
Butter

Generously butter an 8-inch square Pyrex dish.

Pour the sugar into a saucepan, add the lemon juice and 1 cup water, and bring to a boil over low heat, stirring constantly.

When the syrup begins to turn brown, take it off the heat, add the pistachios, and stir.

Pour the mixture into the buttered Pyrex dish, spread it evenly, and cool.

Cut the halva in squares and serve.

Pistachio Cake

Ma'moul

SYRIA

Serves 6

4 cups flour
1¼ cup butter or samn *(mix of butter and olive oil)*
1¼ cup pistachios
1 tsp. baking powder
1 tbsp. orange flower water
1 tbsp. rose water
¾ cup powdered sugar
¾ cup powdered sugar

Sift the flour, then knead it for a long time with the *samn*. Dilute the baking powder in ½ cup warm water, add to the dough, and knead it some more, moistening it from time to time with a little water. Then cover the dough with a clean towel and let it rest for 3 hours.

Chop the pistachios finely and mix them with the powdered sugar, orange flower and rose water.

Roll the dough into small balls, about the size of an egg. Flatten them into patties about ⅛ inch thick. Put a tablespoon of the pistachio paste on each patty and re-form the patties into balls.

Put these balls into a special *ma'moul* mould (for sale in certain Middle Eastern markets) and place the mould in the oven. Bake in preheated 350°F oven about 20 minutes.

As soon as the balls have cooled, sprinkle them with granulated sugar.

II

Logbook

In which Ziryab, like Sindbad, having had a nice voyage, after much thinking about each stage of his travels, pays homage to Arab and neighboring culinary traditions.

Iraq, the mother of all cuisines

Today Iraqi housewives can't afford much to cook with, so I trust you will not hold it against me if I wish to mention *mesguf*, a particularly ingenious method for cooking fish from the Tigris river, or *quzi quçaibi*, the most sumptuous lamb barbecue that humankind has ever invented! As we are waiting for the lifting of the embargo, I would like to tell you what I learned: Five thousand years ago, Iraq had a most varied selection of food products, cereals, legumes, vegetables, aromatic herbs, fruits, meats, fish, shellfish, and mussels. The people knew how to make olive oil, and sesame oil. They knew how to preserve food, make flour for bread, brew beer, and control the required heat for cooking. Jean Bottéro also introduced us to the cuisine of the ancient Babylonians, and was finally able to describe their sophisticated and refined cuisine when he succeeded in deciphering three cuneiform clay tablets, which were written in the early 2000s B.C. in the Akkadian language. Several recipes have impressed me in particular, among others, a pie with little birds. They are first drained in a copper pot, and then left to simmer in an earthenware pot. If there weren't so many onions, leeks and garlic in the recipe, this fantastic dish would still honor the best tables.

Thirty centuries later, during the blessed era, which is known as Islam's Renaissance, Iraq quite naturally found itself at the vanguard of culinary research. In the 10th century C.E., the bibliographer Al-Nadim (d. 995 C.E.) quoted thirteen books with recipes dating back two centuries earlier. Every one of them has unfortunately been lost, including the treatise by the Gourmet Prince, Ibrahim al-Mahdi, who died in 839 C.E. A few recipes of Haroun al-Rachid's half brother, who was himself a paragon of elegance and generosity, were copied in Ibn Sayyar al-Warraq's cookbook, which was written in the late 10th century C.E. and is the oldest cookbook that we have today, and in Baghadi's book, which was written in 1226 C.E. As is often the case, these recipes disclose a certain number of outside influences, in particular from

Persia. This can be seen in Iraq's culinary vocabulary, and their definite inclination for sweet-and-sour dishes. Because of these influences and the large number of ingredients used, because of their interest in rare tastes, and the care with which they insisted on how their food was to be cooked, and presented—sometimes a quest for technical prowess—it is obvious that a grand culinary tradition was developing then, or possibly experiencing another rebirth. Thanks to Ziryab, Muslim Spain had been under Iraq's influence. From there, the message was sent south across to Maghreb, and its many *tadgines* are proof that Maghreb remained more faithful to Iraq than Mashreq itself.

I say this in order to let you know that I have not lost hope: Iraq will some day be reborn from its ashes, and I will have another opportunity to tell you about its cuisine.

Iran, the civilization of rice

There are all sorts of rice. Chinese rice, for instance, has no taste value. It is only meant to supply the toiling masses with the necessary calories for the reproduction of their labor-force. On the contrary, Iranian rice can be counted among the masterpieces of culinary art. This is due, first, to the particular quality of the varieties cultivated in the northern provinces of Gilan and Mazanderan. Alas! *'anbar-boo, darbari*, and *dom-sieh* are not available to most mortals. But, these fantastic varieties would not have existed if the Iranians had not been so consistently dedicated to how they select and cook them. Actually, as I have mentioned previously, their method for cooking rice is unique. It basically consists of washing the rice numerous times, soaking it in salted water for at least two hours, and boiling it until half cooked. You then have to drain it carefully, melt some butter (sometimes with a few drops of water), butter the sides of the pot carefully, and then steam it for forty minutes, first on medium heat, then on very low heat. It is imperative that the top of the pot be covered all around the rim by a clean cloth, so that the steam will not be allowed to escape.

This is called *shelow* rice. It is served with stews, *khorecht*, and *kebabs*, and is sprinkled with *tah-dig*—the layer of golden rice grains from the bottom of the pot. The method is different with *polow* rice. After the first half of its cooking, various other ingredients are added to the rice: meat or fish, vegetables or fruits, herbs and aromatic spices. Both *shelow* and *polow* are light, delicately colored, and soak in the juices and aromas of the ingredients mentioned. No wonder the Iranians look down upon the best Italian *risottos*, and even upon our Near-Eastern rice dishes with lamb or chicken that we have good reasons to be rather proud of. And how could one not dream of the twenty varieties of *polow*, which Jean Chardin in 1670 C.E. was lucky enough to discover, and had the courtesy to inform his contemporaries about?

Today, the Iranians use *sadri* rice for their *shelow* and *polow*. The name comes from the minister who introduced this variety to Iran in the 19th century C.E.—Sadridowleh Mirza Agha Khan. When they run short of it, as we do in France, they settle for India's *basmati* rice, though they will tell you it is not at all the same. No connoisseur will ever deny this, but it is not possible to support the Iranians' claim that their way of cooking rice dates back to the beginnings of time. It was very likely invented in the 16th century C.E., because Muhammad 'Ali Ba'urshi Baghdadi, the author of the first Persian cookbook, did not write one word about it, though he dedicated a large portion to rice, and he wrote his book in 1520 C.E. On the other hand, Ostadh Nurallah, who served at the court of Shah 'Abbas sixty years later, wrote at length about rice in his own book, and about *shelow* and *polow*, giving acceptance of these words in today's terminology. Cyrus the Great has nothing to do with it. The only thing he accomplished in culinary history was to interrupt Balthazar's feast!

Syria, all tastes blended

In Syria, there is one protocol that I would advise you to follow at any cost at all times: when you are in Damascus, never praise the marvelous dishes you enjoyed in Alep, and when in Alep, do not speak of those fabulous dishes that you marveled at in Damascus. These two great cities are particularly proud of their own gastronomies, as much, and sometimes more, than they are of their many thousand years of history, or the proverbial beauty of their women. I am therefore treading at my own risk in meddling in the issue, although I have no other pretension than to add my humble testimony to a case that is far from settled.

First, you should know that Syria—and in this regard, both Damascus and Alep are equals—excel in desserts and pastries. Syria is far ahead of all other countries, including Turkey. Maybe Tripoli, in Northern Lebanon, comes close to Syria, but I tend to think that in Tripoli they use too much sugar. However, there is something I admire even more: it is the seriousness with which the Syrians, or I should say Syrian women, are always looking for the subtlest acid flavors. To do so, they experiment with an incredible variety of products that have no substitute: lemon, vinegar, tomato puree, sumac, tamarind, *verjus*, fermented milk, the green plums of Damascus' Ghouta gardens, and the Morello cherries of the area around Alep.

Taking even more of a risk I might add that Damascus with its *fatte* (*panades*) wins the race by a hair, while Alep dominates all its competitors with its *kebbe* (pounded meat kneaded into bulgur wheat). Alep has at least sixty different recipes. The *kebbe* paste is fried, baked, grilled, or seasoned with a sauce that will convince any gourmet, even one from Damascus, if he is honest enough to admit it, of Alep's manifest superiority. And I am sorry if I have hurt the feelings of my Lebanese friends from Zghorta, Zahle, or the South, but I would add that Alep's superiority also includes raw *kebbe*, as they claim to have the secret for making it. It is said that Alep's women loved to eat it in the *hammams* (baths). Alas! Ingress never stopped there.[1]

Lebanon, innovators at welcoming tables

I have often wondered if the reputation of Lebanese cuisine might not be slightly overrated. After much thinking on the subject, I must say that it is totally justified. True enough, I have had some bad experiences in a few Lebanese restaurants that have sprouted up everywhere in the world the last few years. In the course of my many trips around the world, I too have had the unpleasant opportunity of running across some bad, almost noxious food. And I have suffered from the hands of many bad waiters, even in the best restaurants. They were slow, aggressive, too pressing, or overly slick. But, let me sit down with a genuine *mezze* on my plate, and a glass of genuine *arak*—both Lebanese specialties—and I will forgive the country of the Cedar for its black sheep. All the many appetizers, all the tables loaded with *hors d'œuvre* dishes, the anise liqueurs offered by Turkey or Greece, pale in comparison to what you can find in Lebanon.

I do not think I am overdoing it when I say that their dozens of appetizers, each with their own colors, smells, and tastes, but which together take part in the creation of something new, match perfectly with Lebanon's particular anthropology, geography and history. Yet, Lebanon's appetizers are in no way a summary of the whole Lebanese cuisine. Every region is rightfully proud of one or more of its specialties, from raw *kebbe* in the South, seasoned with basil and marjoram, to Tripoli's sumptuous pastries in the North, to Beirut's *sayyadiyyé*, an Eastern version of Spain's paella, to the incomparable *tabboule* of Mount Lebanon, and they have

[1]Dominique Ingres, (1780-1867) was famous for his paintings representing naked ladies in Turkish baths.

the right to be. All in all, the so-called "Lebanese cuisine" of today is a heritage, which has been passed on with fierce determination from one generation to another, and enriched by Lebanese chefs who have learned from others living in Syria, mostly, but in Egypt as well. And they have immediately "naturalized" these dishes: Lebanese chefs know how to give them an extra touch, which I call, for lack of a better word, "modernistic."

This double skill of assimilation and innovation has eventually given birth to a great reform, which is never commented on: the reform of culinary art in the Near East. As early as in the late 19th century C.E., and without giving up the indispensable friendly ambiance of their *mezzes*, the Lebanese have gradually integrated Western customs, such as the high table and individual plates. It was a Lebanese, Khalil Sarkis, who first took down in writing how to run a kitchen and described the good table manners during a meal, in a book published in Beirut in 1885 C.E. Another Lebanese chef, Al-'Ajami, for decades provided the gourmets in the East with their most memorable gastronomic souvenirs. I still have the taste of his melon sherbet on my tongue, which he served with chilled fruit. May God receive him among His chosen ones!

Palestine, Jaffa oranges

In his *Best Distribution for the Understanding of the Provinces*, the geographer Muqaddasi wrote, "the district of Palestine boasts thirty-six products which can only grow together in that particular place." And he mentioned the pine nut, the quince, the taro, the sycamore, the carob, the wild artichoke, the jujube, the sugar cane, the citron, the bitter orange, the almond, the walnut, the asparagus, the banana, the truffle, several varieties of grapes and figs, and of course, the olive, the date, the apple and the plum, and even the mandrake and the lotus. For those of you who do not know it, Muqaddasi was born in Jerusalem (Al Quds in Arabic), as his name reveals, and he lived in the 10th century C.E., that is, nine centuries before a British Lord, Earl Shaftesbury, a dignified Church of England personality, uttered his double nonsense, which was believed by others, about a land without a people and a people without land.

You will ask me "What about the orange, not the bitter variety, but the acidic orange, the true one—the one that grows in Jaffa?" Well, it is very likely that there was no such orange before the 15th century C.E., maybe even the 16th century, in Palestine, in the other Arab countries, or in Europe, for that matter. It was discovered by the Portuguese in some South Asian islands, and was first transplanted in Portugal and Spain. From there, it was introduced in Italy and France, then along the southern and the eastern shores of the Mediterranean. Thus, it was called in Europe, the "Portuguese orange," or "The orange of Lisbon." In the Arab countries, it was called *burtuqal*, so as not to confuse it with the bitter orange, which was called *narunj*, a Sanskrit word borrowed from Persian. The words in Spanish (*naranja*), Portuguese (*laranja*), and French (*orange*) come from the name *narunj*. To my knowledge, the first time the sweet orange was ever mentioned in Palestine was by the Swedish scholar Fredrick Hasselquist, in 1751 C.E. Since then, the sweet orange has never stopped multiplying: According to an American consul's report written about 1880, Jaffa's orange groves had some eight thousand trees. By then the *shammuti*, the so-called "Jaffa orange," was already served at the best tables in Paris, Vienna, and Saint Petersburg.

As for Palestinian cuisine, the old or the new, you will not be surprised to hear that it tastes just exactly like the cuisine of its neighbors, Syria and Lebanon. It is of course slightly different, because it does not have the typical dishes of either region, but Jerusalem, Hebron, Nablus, or Ako also have their own specialties. I had confirmation of this in Ketty Cattan's beautiful book.[2] There is in it a great recipe for stuffed cucumbers; another for a

---

[2] *Al-Kitab al-hadithl li-'amal al-halwayat wa fann al-tahy* ("The new book of pastries and culinary art")

lentil soup with eggplants, peppers and sour pomegranate juice; and the recipe for *msakhkhan*, which supposedly originated in Jenine, of young fried roosters stuffed with fried onions, pine nuts, and sumac, served over pita breads, sprinkled with olive oil. *Mulukhiyya*, or corete, is also frequently used. The great Egyptian writer, 'Abbas al-'Aqqad, reported eating it during his stay in Jaffa in 1945, and he found it to be excellent. Coming from a man who was not afraid of frequently criticizing his contemporaries, this was no small compliment.

Jordan, king of sheep

The Bedouins in the Near East have a profound connection with the sheep, possibly because they have been living with them ever since the animal was tamed in Mesopotamia some eight thousand years ago. True enough, they have never experienced the exquisite taste of the *pré-salé*[3] lamb, and they do not look forward to a leg of lamb "as though it were a love tryst," as Grimod de la Reynière recommended. Still, Alexandre Dumas explained in the *Grand Dictionnaire de Cuisine* when and where he had the best mutton in all his long gourmet life: it was in 1883 C.E., in Tunisia, not far from the desert. The animal was stuffed with dates, figs, raisins and honey. The natives had cooked it in its skin, covering it up with glowing embers, as is done with a potato or a chestnut.

In Jordan, all aspects of Bedouin values are very highly regarded when invited to eat *mansaf.* This is a dish of which the nomadic shepherds are quite fond. It is a leg or shoulder of lamb, boiled with chopped onions, saffron, paprika, pepper and cinnamon, until it is

[3]This kind of lamb pastures in the meadows along the Atlantic coast of France. The grass is salty from being so close to the ocean.

thoroughly cooked. Some previously boiled fermented ewe's milk is then mixed into the broth. When the yogurt is made with cow's milk, as is the case in France, you have to add one beaten egg white and some flour, and then cook it over medium heat, stirring constantly in one direction with a wooden spoon. *Mansaf* is served like a *panade*: a few slices of bread cut in squares are first laid down at the bottom of the dish, then rice pilaf, and finally the meat and its accompanying sauce. Pine nuts fried in *samn* are then sprinkled on top.

I realize that a lot of French people will hesitate when presented with the most sumptuous *mansaf*, possibly for religious reasons, since the Old Testament forbids "cooking the lamb in its mother's milk," or because yogurt is for them a children's dessert to be eaten when mixed with strawberries or raspberries. They clearly do not know that François 1st of France was cured of his melancholy in 1542 C.E. by eating ewe yogurt, which Suleyman the Magnificent had presented to him as a gift. François the 1st was a great king, one of "the few Frenchmen" who, according to Michelet[4] "ever understood the Eastern question."

The Persian Gulf, palace of spices

The entire aroma of Arabia, Persia and India, have gathered there. Spices are used to season *magbus*, a rice dish—*basmati*, obviously—which is cooked with shrimp, fish, chicken or lamb, in a rather hot sauce, generally with garlic, onions, cilantro, parsley, tomatoes and various spices, and *lumi*, Oman's famous lime (called *numi* in Iraq and Iran), which is sprinkled at the end on top of the dish. Turmeric, ginger, cardamom, and various other spices as well, may be added in subtle mixtures to stews like *shabbat al-rubyan*, exquisite shrimp balls that are cooked in a tamarind sauce. This dish is served with *mhammar* rice, sweetened

[4]Jules Michelet, 1798–1874, a French historian

with date molasses, and seasoned with saffron and cardamom, which have previously been marinated in a spoonful of rose water. Other stews are eaten with *mashkul* rice and fried onions. There are also the *m'addas* with lentils, which must be cooked with basmati rice.

The most astonishing dish in the whole Arabian Peninsula is Saudi Arabian *quzi*. To cook it, you must first clean a 25 pound lamb very well, and one chicken as well. Then salt both, rub them with the usual spices, and some turmeric. Read carefully, it is going to get complicated now: The chicken is to be stuffed with three hard boiled eggs in their shells, some cooked rice, which has previously been seasoned with the same spices, and some shelled almonds, pine nuts, pistachios and raisins. A pinch of saffron, which has macerated in a few drops of rose water, will make your rice even tastier. Truss the chicken and stuff it inside the lamb's stomach, already half sewn up, and fill up the hole with rice. Sew the slit closed, rub the lamb with *samn* and truss tightly. You can then skewer it, and roast it over hot coals. But it is easier to wrap it up in aluminum foil and bake it over medium heat on a rack above the broiler. After two hours, baste it with the juice of the lamb and a little bit of saffroned rose water, and continue to bake the lamb in its aluminum foil for another two hours. Thirty minutes before it is done take off the aluminum foil and baste it copiously. Cut the knots, spread the stuffing onto a large dish, and lay the lamb and the chicken over it. After such a treatment, your honorable guests will not find it difficult to debone it, with their fingers, of course.

In any case, next time you are in one of the countries along the Persian Gulf, do not hesitate to enjoy what is served in private homes, for it is always good cuisine and far from boring—unless you want to condemn yourself to the infamous so-called "international" cuisine, or to sad *mezze* substitutes which no drop of *arak* will of course ever brighten up.

Yemen, a tear for mocha

Yemen is of course coffee and *qat*. I refuse to find out what *qat* might taste like, for I believe that men and women have better things to do in life than chew a wad of green leaves, like goats. As for coffee, which I positively worship, it would not seem right, in fact, it would seem rather preposterous, if I pretended to be able to deal with this subject in a few lines, especially since several scholarly books have recently been printed on the subject. Most of them are written in English, and the authors of *l'Orient des Cafés*[5] were well inspired to learn from them. There is another interesting book I must mention entitled, *Une mémoire pour l'oubli*,[6] written by Mahmud Darwich himself from which you can learn all our tricks for preparing velvety, fragrant and stimulating coffee.

However, I do wish to try and give you a taste of Yemeni cuisine, but you have to know, right off, that it is a festival of spices. There is a typical Yemeni mixture, *hawayij*, made from black pepper, caraway, saffron, cardamom, and turmeric. There is also *zaqq*, a thick sauce made with crushed hot peppers and cilantro, garlic and salt, seasoned with cardamom, pepper and caraway seeds. You dip your bread in it as you eat, as for example with Aden's *hilba*, a dish with fenugreek that has been left to marinate overnight in cold water and crushed garlic, cilantro and hot pepper.

It is customary on Fridays and high holidays to start the meal with very thin bread pancakes, called *bint al-sahn*. They are spread with Eastern style butter (*samn*), piled on top of one another, and baked. They are delicious eaten hot, dribbled with

---

[5] *Coffee and the East*, Koehler, Paris, 1990
[6] *A Memory for Oblivion*, Actes Sud, Arles, 1994

194

butter and honey. The only drawback is that, to be able to digest them, you definitely need a nice cup of mocha, which is supple and full-bodied, and you will not find it in the country! The little mocha that is left after the invasion of *qat* is earmarked for export. This proves that even in gastronomy, no one is a prophet at home.

Egypt, a royal broth

I don't wish to upset my Moroccan friends, but *mulukhiyya* is not okra. In Egypt, where it has been known for ages, as well as in Syria, Lebanon, Palestine and Tunisia, *mulukhiyya* is *Corchorus olitorius*; in French *corète potagère*,[7] or *corète mauve des juifs*.[8] The Fatimids at one time ruled all the countries where it is eaten today. According to some Arabic authors, the reason is that Al-Mu'izz (d. 985 C.E.), the founder of Cairo, consumed a lot of it at the recommendation of his physicians when he arrived to Egypt in ill health after leaving Tunisia. Once healed, he called it *mulukhiyya*, "royal," and it eventually became a favorite food in court. His successors followed his example, and were occasionally rather excessive considering that caliph Al-Hakim (d. 1021 C.E.) decided to ban it from the tables of the poor classes. Which made it even more desirable.

Corete leaves are a very dark green, and can be eaten whole, in a stew. But, this is rarely done in Egypt, where it is usually cooked in a very particular way. The best method that I know common to the Egyptians, the Lebanese and Syrian Christians, consists of preparing a lightly salted and peppered chicken or

[7] Garden Corete
[8] Purple Jewish Corete

rabbit and lamb broth. First, reserve and keep the meat warm, then fry some minced onions in a pot, add a mixture of crushed garlic and salt, cilantro and powdered coriander, continue frying it for a few minutes, then pour part of the broth into it. *Mulukhiyya* should be added to the broth at the last moment. Be sure not to let it cook more than two minutes! One of the five recipes written down by Alep's Ibn al-'Adin (d. 1262 C.E.), even suggests dropping the corete in only when the pot is taken off the fire!

To appreciate this festive dish fully, you have to start by placing toasted pieces of bread in the bottom of a soup tureen, then pilaf rice, the pieces of meat, and pour the broth over it. Finally, you should add a spoon or two of raw chopped onions marinated in vinegar or lemon. It is so good that even those people who are the least receptive to Fatimid esotericism will find it finger licking good.

Tunisia, the date and the olive

The Tunisians are the people of the olive tree. If you will tell me that they are also the people of the date tree, you will also be correct, but it seems to me that their relationship to olive oil is unique. Just think of their very special use of olive oil in their pastries! I recently read a good little book about Tunisian cuisine, and out of fourteen recipes for desserts, eight required olive oil. It is used, for example, to combine the ingredients of *ghrayba*, or coat the *baklava* leaves, or fry *maqrud* or *zlabia* . . . Who could do better? Even the Spaniards, the Italians and the Greeks, who are the three largest producers of olive oil in the world, don't use it as much.

This said, the question is, in Tunisia as anywhere else, will your hosts allow you to keep a little room for the dessert. This is possible if you start your meal with *slata meshuia*—peppers, hot peppers, and tomatoes grilled over a barbecue grill, then peeled, seeded, and crushed with garlic, salt and pepper, and sprinkled, of course, with olive oil. It is still possible if you are then served a fish couscous, mullet, grouper, sea bream, bass, or any other fish, small or large, that is fished along the 800 miles of Tunisian coast. But, if you let yourself be tempted by another Tunisian specialty, 'osbane—sheep andouillette[9]—I doubt that you will be able to make it through to the end. It can be splendid when it is well made, but it is indeed quite filling. Most often, it is cooked in a couscous broth, but it is quite good too as a tadgine or a stew.

I wonder whether I should mention Tunisia's mulukhiyya. It is so very different from what we are used to in the East. Refer to what I wrote about Egypt: I emphasized that corete must not be cooked more than two minutes. But in Tunisia, they make it into a powder and insist on mixing it with olive oil, and letting it simmer for hours with beef, onions, garlic and various spices. My poor mother would have died of indignation just listening to me explain what they do. As far as I am concerned, I would like to quote Ibn Khaldun, himself a child of Tunisia: "Anything that can feed our bodies and is acceptable, eventually becomes a staple food."

Algeria, the celebration of an unknown cuisine

Algerian cuisine is not what you think. Thank God, it has nothing to do with the depressing and repetitive hors d'œuvres that are typically served at those horrendous "King of couscous-type" restaurants. It has nothing to do with the stereotypical couscous, which they drench in a sauce that tastes the same everywhere and is made with tomato paste. If you trust their menus, the only difference between the various couscous dishes is the name of the meat they use! Where are the marvelous kesksu with fresh fava beans and green peas, with wild or cultivated artichokes, with dried legumes, with squash and milk, with a stuffed sheep paunch, and lavender blossoms, each seasoned with the proper spices? What has been done with the date or raisins mesfuf, the dried or preserved meat t'ams? And why are they hiding from us other members of the cereal family, what the French call "les petits

[9]A type of sausage made from sheep intestines

plombs": *mhamsa*, or *"les gros plumbs"*: *berkukes*, and even cracked barley: *butchish*, the oldest of them all?

You should know that, over the centuries, and in spite of the many historical vicissitudes, or rather, because of them, several of the better culinary traditions have been combined in Algeria. To the old Berber base, already rich with all the bounty found along the Mediterranean basin—with olives in the North and dates in the South—the know-how of Baghdad, Cordoba, and Istanbul appeared on the scene. Then products that were hitherto unknown were introduced, some from the East, thanks to the Arabs (durum wheat, rice, the eggplant, and spinach), others from the West, thanks to the *Moriscas*, who were expelled from Spain and who introduced South American products (like the tomato, pepper, and potato). This is why you will find in people's homes, and sometimes in cookbooks as well, a highly varied Algerian cuisine. Their soups, salads, couscous, stews, *keftas* (lamb sausage), and the pastries especially, are as good as their Western neighbor's where the sweet *tadgines*, which go back to Medieval Arab cuisine, are alongside the Ottoman *dolmas* and *büruks*. Paradoxically, France's influence, in this cuisine, is very superficial. Of course, the French have introduced wine, but I have nothing to say in praise of *Sidi-Brahim*.[10]

I must inform you that I am utterly puzzled by the very poetic and sometimes comic names of many Algerian recipes. I have often heard about them but have never had the opportunity to actually taste them. I am thinking of the "Bey among His People," the "Baby in His Mother's Lap," "My Uncle's House," or the "Wrapped One in Its Own Wrap," which I believe is very mysterious. I have been dreaming for years about a medlar[11] *tadjine*, but I am afraid to cook it myself. Is there among my readers an Algerian woman with a big heart and nimble fingers who is ready to help me?

[10] *Sidi-Brahim* is a very heavy red wine that lacks in French finesse . . .

[11] Medlar is a small juicy fruit that resembles a smooth skinned apricot with a double pit, and a delicate, somewhat sour and bitter taste.

Morocco, where the gourmets can take a rest

Is it possible to speak of Moroccan cuisine without using and abusing the superlative form? Let us begin with *harira*, the family dish *par excellence* where the healthy rusticity of the legumes combines with a very sophisticated preparation. It would be sheer dishonesty to deny that this soup is simply the best in the world. Consider *bastella*, a crusty sweet, peppered puff pastry filled with pigeon and almonds. I very much doubt that there are many dishes in all of French or Chinese cuisines that can be compared to it. And I will repeat the same about certain fruit and honey *tadgines*, or about another marvel of exquisite refinement, *qammama*. It calls for caramelized onions and is seasoned with cinnamon. I do not have enough room here to give you its recipe, but you should know that anybody can cook it. And this is not the smallest merit of Moroccan cuisine: its very strictly codified general principles allow for a multiplicity of combinations. This is why, from one generation to the other, each family has produced splendid chefs.

For me, a stranger from the East, Morocco first tastes of saffron. This spice, with its very particular taste, stands like a king among his subjects, and they are more numerous there than anywhere else. Only good chefs master how to mix or use the right proportion of this royal spice. Nowhere else in the world can we find the incredible variety of pastries. Some, like *fidawsh*, date back to Andalusia's 13th century C.E., as Ibn Razin already knew of it. Nowhere in the world are the pancakes and the galettes more varied, some probably go back to the old Berber tradition. But, my main cause for surprise and enchantment is the combination of the sweet and the savory, which we gave up in the East after the 16th century C.E. All the *tadgines*, which use fruit or sweet vegetables, such as the red squash and the sweet potato, seasoned with saffron, ginger, pepper, cinnamon, honey and orange flower water, are just simply sublime. As far as the stuffing is concerned, I still prefer rice to couscous, possibly because I am used to it. In any case, it seems to me the stuffing is not so important in Moroccan cuisine, though their honey chicken *m'ammar* is excellent.

Now is the time for me to praise Fatema Hal's beautiful book, *Les Saveurs et les Gestes*. It was published at the right time to celebrate what must be called "Moroccan Civilization" through its cuisine. I was personally touched by her affectionate description of the *dadas*, those Black women who gave so much to Moroccan cuisine. Fatema Hal is totally right in chastising those who ignore such a rich tradition, and she is right in focusing on the regional varieties. She tries to convince her fellow Moroccans that gastronomy nowadays cannot remain within the confines of our houses. This proves that we, the Arabs, from the Near East to the Far West, have exactly the same battle to fight.

Spain, a perfume from Paradise

It is not easy to pay homage to Muslim Spanish cuisine after the excellent book written by Lucie Bolens on the subject. You will find everything in it, all written in a beautiful style, which really does no harm to the content. Is there indeed a more attractive country for this research of mine? Spain is blessed by God. The olive oil flows freely. Durum wheat, which was probably introduced during the 10th century C.E. can live, supposedly, up to one hundred years. There is an abundance of fruits and vegetables, cereals and legumes, those that have always grown locally, as well as those which came later from across the seas. The meat and fish are excellent. And for at least four centuries, the Mediterranean way of life was able to develop freely, in particular in the art of eating, from agriculture to gastronomy. Very few countries have been allowed to have so much in so little time.

The Andalusians were people of taste, and they unwittingly answered our legitimate curiosity. Since they left us with many traces of their culture, we now feel that we know many things about who they really were from their treatises on agronomy, like the one of Toledo's Ibn Bassal (11th century C.E.) or Seville's Ibn al-'Awwam (12th century C.E.), the botany compendium by Malaga's Ibn al-Baytar (d. 1248 C.E.), as well as their calendars, recipe books, etc. Bolens mentioned two of these several times. Both date back to the 13th century C.E.: *Ornements de la Table* by Murcia's Ibn Razin, and a fantastic book whose author is unknown, a genuine treasure on the subject. She studied them at great length, and even partly translated them. Neither is limited to Andalusia. They are indeed remarkable, because of what they have to say about ingredients, and ways to combine them. But their main interest lies in what they present to us: a very early manifestation of cultural universalism.

This praise takes nothing away from another Andalusian character, Ibn al-Azraq, who was born in Malaga. His knowledge in matters of the law was apparently as comprehensive as his priggish love for food. A disciple and commentator of Ibn Khaldun, he left for Egypt in 1487 C.E. after the fall of his native city to the Christians. He went to plead for Sultan Quaybay's help which evidently was not granted. Like his master, he worked as a Turkish judge in Cairo, then in Jerusalem, where he died in 1491 C.E. In the meantime, he had the opportunity of writing a piece of poetry in which he bitterly lamented the loss of Al-Andalus, in particular, its unmatched couscous and unequalled donuts, which proves that gourmets are ardent patriots in their own way . . .

France, Hell for cattle

While he was staying in Paris from 1826 to 1831 C.E., the unquestionable pioneer of Arab Renaissance, Rifa'a al-Tahtawi was not just interested in studying Montesquieu[12] and Sylvestre de Sacy,[13] but also other aspects of France's everyday life: the Parisians' eating habits and their table manners. What he wrote in his famous memoirs is worth investigating, for his was definitely the first Arab incursion in the kitchens of France.

Evidently, Rifa'a was not what we call a gourmet. In spite of his universal curiosity, you will not find a single allusion to Antonin Carême (a Parisian chef) in his book, though Carême was at the head of a real culinary revolution at the time. Still, the young sheikh of al-Azhar's Egypt's Islamic University conscientiously noted anything that he thought might be helpful to his contemporaries. It is thanks to him that the Egyptians learned that the Parisians always had to have bread at their meals, that they drank wine without necessarily getting drunk, that their meals were very varied, even among the poorer classes, and that there were places called "restaurants locanda" where it was possible to eat at least as well as at home. As for the kind of meals they ate, let's say that, as a good Egyptian, Rifa'a remained loyal to his country's cuisine. I do not mean to hurt anybody's feelings, but he judged that the cuisine of the Francs was tasteless, as well as were their fruits, except for their local peaches. Rifa'a even wrote in verse an outright attack against his hosts in the margin of his Arabic translation of Georges-Bernard Depping's *Aperçu Historique sur les Mœurs et les Coutumes des nations*, calling them "chicken stiflers" and "eaters of fish with their guts still inside." But his patriotism did not prevent him from appreciating, even quietly recommending, the table manners of the

[12]Charles de Secondat, Baron de Montesquieu, (1669–1755), French Magistrate and writer. The founder of Political Sciences, he initiated the theory of the three powers (legislative, executive and judicial).

[13]Antoine Isaac, baron Silvestre de Sacy (1765–1838), a specialist of the Arab world.

Francs, such as their use of the individual plate, and their meal of several dishes served one after the other. All in all, long before Brigitte Bardot, the only thing that really shocked him was the treatment which the French inflicted upon the animals in their slaughterhouses. After seeing what was going on there, Rifa'a's servant thanked God for "not having made him a cow in the country of the Francs!"

With all of Rifa'a's fascination and prejudices, no 19th century Arab traveler, not even a traveler in the 20th century, would have anything to add, except that a few professional chefs, mainly Egyptians, might bring back from France some recipes for their westernized clients. Something else—it is astonishing to see that, although Ahmad Faris al-Shidyaq (1801–1887 C.E.) who was rightly considered "the Arabic Rabelais,"[14] never spoke of French cuisine in Rabelais-like terms. Actually, he satisfied himself by recalling his wife's injurious comments on the subject. It appears as if the sexual mores of the French, men and women, which he apparently studied at a very close angle, had exhausted all his energy . . .

Italy, the origin of pasta

The *Larousse Gastronomique* insists on trying to convince us that the recipes of the *spaghetti, lasagne* and *tagliatelle* came from China, and were brought back by Marco Polo. Yet, no one can deny that the Italians knew about it before the famous Venetian came back from his long trip, in 1215 C.E. This does not prevent the Koreans from claiming that they invented pasta, or the Armenians from pretending that spaghetti is derived from some long, thin strips of dough, which their ancestors were crazy about, or the Lithuanians from trying to prove that pasta was eaten along the Baltic long before Jesus Christ ever came to save the world. What can the

[14]François Rabelais (1494–1553), a writer, monk, and physician. He specialized in tales highlighting the pleasure of all senses.

Arabs say in the middle of this free-for-all? Well, we could always speak about much more serious things!

First, I will never tire of saying so, but real *maccheroni*, like real couscous, are unthinkable with anything other than durum wheat. The chemists can explain it better than I could, as they insist on the eminent role of gluten, which can be found in large quantities in this particular type of wheat. Thus, it is not surprising that pasta and couscous appeared on the scene at about the same time, between the 11th and the 13th centuries C.E. Or that the two events took place along the same tropic, and in the Western part of the Mediterranean at that. It is not generally known that it was an Andalusian Arab, Ibn Razin, who first wrote on the subject around 1250 C.E. He even placed the two in the same chapter! You should read what he wrote about *fidawsh*, small pasta that was left to dry in the sun. The Christian Spaniards borrowed it for their generic name for pasta—*fideos*. And it is even less known that the Italians first called it *aletria*, an Arabic word derived from the Aramean, with its article—*al-itriya*. Firuzabadi, an Arab lexicographer of the 14th century C.E., said that the word was used for "a food that looks like threads, made with flour."

I might be tempted to say that our ancestors the Arabs invented pasta, or else, that they greatly contributed to it. But I will not say so, out of modesty, and sympathy for Italy.

Greece, the forgotten splendor of Byzantium

People like Bashshar ibn Burd and Abu Nuwas, who might prefer Chiraz wine to camel's milk, are not necessarily Shu'ubites. Neither are those who claim that medieval Arab cuisine owes much, if not the most essential, to Persia. Just by scanning through the cuisine treatises that I have been mentioning here, anybody can see that the names of the various ingredients, preparations, liaisons, and dishes, all originated in Persia. Some of these names have since disappeared or fallen into oblivion, but most of them still remind us, at each meal, of our cultural debt. Yet, our ancestors owe another debt of gratitude to the Greeks, more precisely to Byzantium, which they were not quite unaware of. Old Greece was our first mentor. It allowed our Umeyyad caliphs to fill their plates sumptuously, and Greece was probably our last mentor at that, for the Greek influence continued throughout the Ottoman Empire.

If we searched for a reason for this ingratitude of our stomachs we would find it in the history of the tumultuous relationship between Byzantium and Islam over the centuries. Of course, this does not apply to Ancient Greece, the Arabs freely acknowledge its grandeur and had no problem assimilating Greek philosophy and sciences. Actually, every time the Arab scholars dealt with cuisine, in particular the theory of the humors, they would pay homage to the Greek physicians and botanists. Basically, the Greeks were called upon to bring us their precious guarantee every time anybody needed some scientific confirmation. But until the fall of Constantinople, Byzantium remained Islam's most intimate enemy. Because it was much too close, Byzantium was the empire that they vanquished but were not able to defeat—the only power, since Heraclius, which would not tolerate Islam, and that Islam could not tolerate. Their mutual enmity could only end with the disappearance of one of the two. This is why, as André Miquel explained, the Arab geographers of the classical age reduced Byzantium to a powerful State, at least superficially, but without people, plants, animals, or everyday life. Consequently, it did not have a cuisine, although a geographer or two curiously mentioned the Byzantines' skills for cooking.

As for the Ottoman period, it would indeed seem difficult to believe that the warlike Turks did not assimilate Byzantium's culinary traditions as much as they later influenced Greek cuisine. But the Arabs have a tendency to forget this, and to attribute their Ottoman heritage only to the Turks. Very few Iraqis know that their *tibsi* (baked dishes) are derived from the Greek *tapsi* (a tin baking dish), and not many Syrians would seriously accept or consider the hypothesis that Alep's famous *karabidj* indirectly comes from Byzantium's *kurabiedes*. As for the Moroccans, who were never part of the Ottoman empire, I have no idea

why, but they probably called their sublime pigeon puff pastry *bastella*, from the Greek *pistella*, which for the Byzantines was a flat bread cake with sesame and honey. This cake was so delicious that, according to malicious gossip, St. John Chrysostomes would eat it before Holy Communion!

Turkey, the empire of the senses

The question about the existence of a great Turkish cuisine is often asked. This is debatable. Yet, there is indeed a great Ottoman cuisine. And the distance between the two is not only chronological. The former suggests an ethnic identity. It is bound to be limited, repetitive, and narrow. However, the latter evokes a huge empire. It is the work of various peoples: Turks, Greeks, Arabs, Armenians, Kurds, and the many people of the Balkans and Caucasus, as well as the Sephardic Jews, who, after their expulsion from Spain by the Catholic kings, found refuge in the Islamic lands. This culinary mixture does not need much commentary. Just sit down to a *mezze*, in a restaurant in Saloniki, Ankara, Alep or Beirut, and you will notice at once that three fourths of those small dishes are the same everywhere, and that their nuances are very slight indeed. And, as Raymond Queneau (the French writer) once noticed, the glasses around you do not have the red color of wine, but the white color of *arak*.

I was recently thinking about this nostalgically, as I was leafing through the latest book on the subject. In spite of its inadequate title, it does lead one back to the Ottoman tradition because it is not afraid to point out what the Turks owe to all the others: Istanbul's spice market, a souvenir of times past, is described as an "Egyptian-like" *Kasar*; Turkey's ewe cheese is Andalusian, and the Sephardic Jews brought it back; and the Turks eat Circassian chickens, a Persian rice dish, an Albanian liver dish, and many Greek, Armenian, or Arab dishes, which do not try to hide their origins. But in return, anybody can see how much we owe Turkey for its yogurt, *dolma* (stuffed vegetables), *bürek* (puff pastry), and *kebab, lahmacun* (pizzas)—unless some of these dishes are medieval Arab cuisine, which would have been inspired by Persia.

In our times of tribal, ethnic, and religious madness, I cannot think of a better antidote than this imperial culture. Thanks to gastronomy, I have no fear of saying it: in many ways, Ottomanism is humanism.

Cyprus, Aphrodite's goats

The blonde, bathing ladies from the North, once English and Swedish, and today Slavic, getting a lazy tan in the sun of Aphrodite's island, are evidently not interested in the best that Cyprus has to offer: its dairy products and its wine. This is too bad, for when I was in Cyprus, there were so many things to absorb, that I did not know where to start! On the one hand, there were the ewes, goats and vineyards, calling me toward the hills, and on the other hand, I felt strongly attracted to the foreign and full round curves of the ladies who were bronzing themselves on the beaches of Ayia Napa. What a cruel dilemma I was in!

Still, I was able to dedicate several very pleasant days to the wines of Cyprus, more precisely, to the famous *Commanderie*,[15] which I knew to have the oldest *apellation* in the world. Hesiod already praised it in the 8th century C.E., and it has become what it is today, after Richard the Lionhearted conquered the island and then sold it to the Templars in 1191 C.E.. The fame of *Commanderie* wine has continued to spread, and some contend, though it is quite unlikely, that it was the origin of three sublime wines: Spain's *madeira*, Italy's *marsala* and Hungary's *tokay*.

[15]The Commanderie of the Order of the Templars, at the time of the Crusades

What is certain, though, is that it does taste like Andalusia's *jerez*, since it is, like *jerez*, brought to maturity in a row of vats and arranged according to aging time. Every time that some older wine is drawn, the vat is filled with the wine from the vat next to it; which in turn, is filled with a younger wine, and so on. In this way, each generation is taking the care to mature the one that follows.

Whatever its personal quality, though, I must say that *Commanderie* first attracted me because of its eminent role in the history of the Near East. It is said that Sultan Selim II, a.k.a. "the Souse," only decided to conquer Cyprus in 1570 C.E. because he wanted to drink his fill. But while he was guzzling down *Commanderie*, Europe was preparing her revenge, and so came the catastrophe of Lepante one year later. The general who had conquered the island, Lala Mustapha Pasha, was later appointed governor of Damascus, and his descendants are many. I personally know one of his great-great-grandchildren. He is, like me, a food critic.

III

Gourmet Lexicon

In which Ziryab mentions other fruits and vegetables,
as well as dishes, beverages, and historical characters,
that every gourmet should know.

A for Asparagus

Cut off a few ram's horns, and plant them in the dirt, soon after that, you will get some nice asparagus! This strange belief was uttered by the Andalusian botanist Ibn al-Baytar, quoting Galen and Dioscorides and had something to do with propagating the attractive reputation of the asparagus as an aphrodisiac, a legend that originated in Antiquity. Of course, the reputation is totally undeserved and a good many people have been quite disappointed. The legend could be referring to the vegetable's shape, not its substance.

It would be better to eat your asparagus for the sake of eating them, without any expectations of their sexual benefits This, in itself, will bring you much enjoyment. But you must cook them very simply, just peeled and boiled for a short time in hot salted water and serve them with a sauce that would enhance their delicate taste. The most common sauce is vinaigrette, but like Fontenelle,[1] you might prefer melted butter combined with a chopped hard-boiled egg. The taste of an egg goes well with asparagus. The Arabs realized this very early on, as can be seen in Ibn al-'Adim's treatise, which has been mentioned many times in this book. But I do not like the other classical Arab recipes, from Andalusia or the East. They smother the taste of the asparagus under a mass of ingredients. I am also not too fond of the warlike accents of the 'Abassi poet Kushajim, who by comparing the asparagus to a spear, did a disservice to the asparagus, to the spear and to poetry.

[1]Bernard de Fontenelle (1657–1757). A French writer, he was at the origin of the Enlightenment.

B for *Baqlawa*

Although the word, and probably the dish, is Turkish, there is no comparison between the *baqlawa* (or *baklava*) made in Istanbul, and those made in Alep, Damascus, Beirut, or Tripoli. Outside of the golden square of these four cities, the pastry is often mistreated. A *baqlawa* is a set of very thin dough leaves layered on top of each other, stuffed with chopped walnuts, roasted and chopped almonds, or much better, pistachios. It is then cut into squares or parallelograms, smeared with *samn* and baked. Once it is cooked, *baqlawa* must be sprinkled, not with honey, which makes it too heavy to digest, but with lighter sugar syrup.

Iran's *baghlava* belongs to the same family, and is quite as delicious, but it does not have the consistency or the taste of its Ottoman cousins. It has two layers of almonds and pistachios, and is seasoned with cardamom, and this makes all the difference to us Mediterranean people.

B for Beans

When he wrote about *lubiya*, toward the end of the 11th century C.E., Sevilla's Abu al-Khayr, the author of *The Guide of the Plants for the Physicians*, explained that he personally knew of eleven varieties. Yet, not one could have belonged to the family of *Phaseolus vulgaris*, which is what we call "beans" today. The reason is simple: *Phaseolus vulgaris* came to us from America in the 16th century C.E., along with the potato and the tomato, and it took a couple of centuries for it to be accepted in Europe, followed by the southern and eastern parts of the Mediterranean. So what was Abu al-Khayr talking about? He was very likely describing other members of the fava bean family, possibly the hyacinth beans, which Razes and Avicenne, and Dioscorides before him, had mentioned in their treatises.

What makes things even more complicated is that both legume families have a lot in common. Both species have pods that must be shelled, and the *lubiya* seeds, which Abu al-Khayr mentioned, were sometimes kidney shaped, like the beans from America. Addionally, some varieties of *lubiya* can be eaten green, as whole pods and seeds, exactly like string beans. Abu al-Khayr explained that they were very popular for their diuretic properties, for their use in Eastern and Spanish dishes, and because they were delicious. Alep's Ibn al-'Adim used ashes or an alkaline solution to make their green color stand out, and he seasoned them with caraway and cilantro. Once they were cooked, he added an acid taste, with some lemon or some pomegranate juice, *verjus* or sumac. There is also another similarity between hyacinth beans and ordinary beans: When they are dry and remain for sometime in our bellies, they express their ill feelings in a very loud way. But then, Razes explained that savory and cumin could make them more polite.

C for Coriander

❖

The fanatics of coriander, of which I am one, hate the ridiculous name it has been given. It is more or less the same in most European languages. It comes from the Greek "*koris*," which means "bug," supposedly because of its cute little umbelliferous flower, which is so dear to the hearts of the Arab, Indian and Chinese people, and is supposed to emanate the same kind of smell as the aforementioned bug. But what is especially unbearable to me is that the people who believe these lies then spread them around with a puckered face, although they have probably never seen, smelled, nor tasted one single leaf of coriander.

In order to convert my French friends, who are open-minded people, I usually suggest that they try a genuine masterpiece of Moroccan cuisine called *harira*, which is impossible to cook without coriander, much like Iraq's okra stew, which is very popular, or Lebanon's *mulukhiyya*, or the fresh fava beans, which the Syrians are crazy about and cook as a stew with olive oil, rice and *bulgur*. Better still, before you make a final decision about coriander, why not replace parsley with coriander when you cook mussels or scallops? I am sure that this will convince you, and then you will understand why I am so proud when the French call cilantro "Arab parsley."

D for *Dolma*

❖

For the Turks, anything that is stuffed is *dolma*, including a sheep's paunch or tripe. For the Arabs, who borrowed the name, *dolmas* are only vegetables. Since the vegetables that can be stuffed are quite numerous, *dolmas* constitute a large part of our cuisine.

How is one to tackle the subject? I favor a classification, which takes into consideration the type of vegetable, the type of filling, or the liquid in which *dolmas* are cooked. First, consider vegetables, which can be hollowed out, like the zucchini and the eggplant, and those that are rolled up, like the leaves of the grapevine, chard or cabbage. Except for the pepper, both categories require some skills. I know some people who are skilled, and others who are not. There is another difference when considering type of stuffings used, it depends on whether people use meat or not. With some stuffings, meat is added with rice (or sometimes with *bulgur*), but it may also, especially when using yogurt, be the only ingredient used, except for chopped onion and fried pine nuts. Still others make stuffing with rice and chopped onions, which must be fried in olive oil; and the vegetable *dolma* is then left to cook in a tomato sauce, with raisins, pine nuts, and cinnamon. Finally, depending on whether the *dolmas* use meat or not, they require a tomato sauce with tamarind or water, with or without some lemon juice. And, when yogurt is used, it is only added at the very last moment.

These are very well balanced, typically family dishes, "bourgeois dishes," as the French say. No wonder the large cities in the East compete for the honor of having invented them, and each claims to have the specific secret for cooking them. The city-dwellers unashamedly assume that the country people and the nomads are too boorish to appreciate the finesse of the dish. There is a famous story of a Bedouin, who, being offered a dish of stuffed zucchini, refuses it, saying: "If your rice was half-decent, you wouldn't have tried to conceal it!"

F for *Fuqqa*

❖

Fuqqa is one of the names for beer in classical Arabic, along with *mizr, ja'a, ma'al-sha'ir*, but it seems to me that pronouncing it is enough to evoke the frizzy, foaming beverage. It was already known in pre-Islamic Arabia, where various cereals were used to make it, like barley among others. But *fuqqas* were never drunk as such. They were salted, or sweetened, usually with honey. Sometimes, they were both sweet and salty. Many spices were added, cinnamon, ginger, cloves, pepper, or several herbs (tarragon, rue, or mint). Since there were no hops, the Egyptian gourmets who were looking for a bitter drink would use lupin, or else corete, the famous *mulukhiyya*, which the Fatimid caliph Al-Hakim tried to ban for reasons which had nothing to do with drinking beer.

This said, it is wine, of course, and not beer, or any other alcoholic beverage, that contributed most to the merriment of our ancestors. Though classical Arab literature does mention brewers at great length (*faqqa'*, or *fuqqa'i*), or what the *kizan* (the brewing vats) looked like (*kizan* is the plural form for *kuz*). However, there are only a dozen short poems about the drink itself, and they all, in a roundabout way, urge people to prefer wine!

I for Ibrahim ibn al-Mahdi

It would be unthinkable not to include the prince of gourmets, Ibrahim ibn al-Mahdi (779–839 C.E.) in this Lexicon, for he wrote the first cookbook in the Arabic language. His recipes were varied and detailed, and very modern for his time. The book has unfortunately been lost, but some forty recipes did manage to survive. They were passed on by his successors, and were eventually collected by a mysterious Andalusian genius in the 13th century C.E. whom I will discuss later.

The son, brother, and uncle of caliphs, at a time when the Caliphate was very powerful, Ibrahim had no interest in power, except when forced by circumstances. He much preferred dealing with good food, and with poetry and music. He had an extraordinary chef at his side, Badi'a, a woman who had been given to him by his elder brother Harun al-Rashid. She too would deserve a whole chapter in culinary history, which unfairly almost never takes women into account.

You can read about this peculiar Abassid prince in David Waines' beautiful book *The Cuisine of the Caliphs*, which renders him justice. As far as I am concerned, I believe he made one faux pas: He once served Harun al-Rashid, who was shocked, a dish of fish tongues, in the shape of a fish. This was an idea for a decadent Roman, not for an Arab of the Golden Age.

J for Jujube

In Islam, the most sublime of all the trees is the incomparable, the unique *sidrat al-muntaha*, the Jujube tree of the Frontier. When the Prophet ascended to the Heavens, the angel Gabriel showed him the way, and since there was a point at a jujube tree, where Gabriel himself could not go further, he told the Prophet to continue on by himself, still closer to God. This is why the jujube tree symbolizes the frontier; the eschatological place which separates what may and what may not be known. Evidently, this responsibility weighs heavily on our earthly jujube trees, and why they find it hard to exist today. The few that remain produce the juice that is used to manufacture soothing lozenges for our sore throats. And, if it were not for their juice production, they would no longer exist. And that's too bad.

The jujube berry is a delicate fruit, which strangely enough, looks like an olive, and is in some way, inseparable from our human existence. According to a *hadith* of the Prophet, it was Adam's first food, not in Paradise of course, but on earth. Many varieties grow in areas that stretch from China to the Mediterranean. However, the best variety is, what we in the Near East call *'unnab*. Its berries are red and sweet. According to Pliny, the Romans discovered it in Syria, at the time of Augustus. They introduced it to Italy, then to Tunisia, and then to Spain. And in the meantime, they created the worst use for it when they braided it into nasty thorns for Jesus of Nazareth. Another variety, which produces North Africa's lotus, is famous too, though it is not cultivated. This was the terrible food of the Lotus-eaters, who were mentioned in the *Odysseus*. Like Ulysses' companions, anyone who eats it eventually forgets his mother country.

In the Middle Ages, our ancestors' memories remained unscathed, although they ate the jujube berry in any manner they liked, even with lamb or fish. But it was with *khubz al-abazir*, the Arab gingerbread, with walnuts and almonds, that the jujube gave us its very best. Our ancestors also used it as a soft beverage to quench their thirst, or as a hard drink, to lead them back to the Garden of Eden.

K for *Kunafa*

The word is quite old, although you will not find it in Jawhari's, Firusabadi's or Ibn Mansur's dictionaries. But you will see it in the cookbook of Ibn Razin, who lived in Andalusia, and in the cookbook of Ibn al-'Adim, who was a Syrian. Evidently, for them it was some kind of a pastry, and it looked more like a *baqlawa*, than the *kunafa* that we eat today. Other literary sources also mention it, but in spite of their interesting comments about the history and geography of *kunafa*, they do not give any precision as to why and how the look of it changed. The Egyptian poet Jazzar (d. 1280 C.E.), who was a butcher, as his name shows, had nothing to say about the pastry itself, and he wasted his talent by only alluding to the sweet syrup that was used on it. The only thing we can infer from another poet, Ibn 'Unayn (d. 1233 C.E.), a Syrian who was not ordinarily afraid of calling a spade a spade, is that *kunafa* was different from *qata'if*, a thick pancake made with some leavened dough. Had his thick book on pastries not been lost to us, the polygrapher Suyuti would have been in a position to tell us more on the subject. At any rate, it is thanks to him, from another book, that we know the story of Mu'awiya: On the advice of his physician, the first Umeyyad caliph, Muhamad ibn Athal, would eat *kunafa* during the month of Ramadan, in order to calm his insatiable hunger.

Today's *kunafa* is close to what our ancestors called "*itriya*," which means "dough threads." *Kunafa* apparently has not had this borrowed name for a long time, for the great dictionary *Taj al-'Arus*, which dates back to the 18th century C.E. gives quite another meaning to the word. But this short period of time was enough for it to get to the very top of Eastern cuisine. It is torn to shreds, then spread on the table, then rolled, and finally stuffed with cheese, cream, nuts and pistachios. Too bad for Mu'awiya, caliph though he was, if his *kunafa* was different!

L for Lentils

❖

It is said that an alleged reported *hadith* had claimed that seventy prophets had blessed the lentil. But, in his *Prophet's Medicine*, the great Hanbali Law Doctor, Ibn Qayyim al-Jawziyya, claimed that this *hadith* was apocryphal: He mentioned the flat denial of an early *traditionist* who heard what was said, and denied the words in writing. I wish, though, that the venerable magistrate had been less immersed in his scholarly demonstrations, and had spent some time considering the man who forged the *hadith*. This man was so much in love with the lentil that he went so far as to sacrifice his own reputation here on earth, and the salvation of his soul in the hereafter.

Actually, nobody in history has ever shown so much concern for this smallest of all legumes. The Bible says that Esau exchanged his birthright for a "roux" of lentils. But this was a deliberate decision, as he was literally starving to death. As for the Athenian Cynicists, who appreciated the frugality of the lentils very much—well, they were cynicists. Later, the Syrian emperor Heliogabalus, the most debauched of all, would actually sprinkle his lentils with precious gems. That was the reason why Antonin Artaud, some eighteen centuries later, called him "a crowned anarchist." All things considered, our anonymous forger is the only one who ever tried to defend the cause of the lentils. And this was quite risqué, for all the physicians of his time, even the wisest ones, had united against the lentil. It was accused of thickening our blood, and of engendering melancholy diseases, even cancer.

Fortunately, neither the physicians, nor the lawyers, were successful in convincing our ancestors to steer away from their *mujaddara, rashta* and *'adasiyya*. These dishes are still eaten today: *Mujaddara* combines lentils with rice or *bulgur, rashta* calls for pasta, and *'adasiyya* (under another name) for chard. This is very wise, because the combination is both healthy, and very tasty. As for the combination of lentils and *namaksud*, salted meat, which the same physicians condemned vigorously, we know that it has become very popular in other climates, and there is no reason why it should not be the case with us, too. We would only have to substitute mutton for pork.

M for *Mezze*

Having recently had the opportunity to enjoy excellent *mezzes* in Turkey, Greece and Cyprus, I wish to repeat, insist and confirm that Lebanon is to *mezze* what Italy is to pasta, Iran to rice, and Japan to *sushi*. In Lebanon there is something special—a greater diversity and generosity, a special know-how, and no doubt, the typical exuberance of the Near East. Perhaps this is why Lebanon is unique.

But the Lebanese are wrong in claiming that all of these *hors d'œuvre* originated in Lebanon, as if you could only excel in an art or science that you yourself had invented. They are wrong too in not trying to keep up with the times. I believe that they ought to study what is going on around them, which they did until recently. There is a lot to be learned from Greece, and even more from Spain's *tapas*, in particular the ones made with fish and shellfish. And something else: there is no reason to look to the Turks or the Persians for the origin of the word *mezze*, or *maza*, as it is pronounced in the Near East. In his *Lisan al-'Arab*, which dates back to the 14th century C.E., Ibn Mansur explained that one word for wine is *muzza*, or *mazza*, because it is *"muzz,"* both sweet and sour. And the word *tamazzuz* means "to sip wine." Maybe this is just a coincidence, and there are a few of them in the history of words and dishes, but for me, a fervent admirer of Lebanese *mezze*, this is quite a lucky coincidence . . .

N for *Nabidh*

❖

In most Arab countries today, the word "*nabidh*" means "wine."
It used to be quite a different beverage, which was made by mac-
erating grapes, dates, or other fruits for some time in water. The
Prophet himself loved it. According to the most authentic *hadith*,
he never let the fruit macerate longer than three days. But such a
beverage tends to ferment quickly in the heat, and a furious con-
troversy developed among Muslim lawmakers, about whether or
not it was licit to drink it. For most of them, the Malikites, the
Shafi'ites, and the Hanbalites, as well as the Shi'i Muslims, it was
not permitted, and those who drank *nabidh* were to be punished
with forty or eighty lashes, just like those who drank wine. On
the other hand, the Hanafites were nice enough to authorize this
drink under certain conditions. And the Mu'tasilites—Jubba'i
among them believed that the faithful could drink it as much as
they liked in order to get familiarized on earth with the pleasures
awaiting them in the Hereafter.

Cadi Waki, who died in 812 C.E., was one of those who favored
nabidh. His legendary piety was well known, and he did not
deprive himself of drinking it. It is said that after studying and
teaching the *hadith*, he would walk home for supper, then spend
the night praying and drinking until he finished his ten *ratl* a day.
On certain occasions, he would continue teaching late into the
night, but he would then ask his students to supply him with
nabidh. And, when he ran out of the drink, he would blow the
candle out, saying: "Give me more, and I'll give you more!"

O for Onion

◈

Islam is "the religion of the fragrant breath," as Lucie Bolens so nicely puts it. No wonder the onion is not considered very highly with us. By order of the Prophet, those who ate it were denied access to the Mosque. But this decision, evidently, only concerned the raw onion. By eating it without restraint, the faithful were deliberately condemning themselves out of the community. When it is cooked, the onion is definitely innocent. It is indispensable in the kitchen, it helps in medicine, and it is appreciable for reviving the flame of exhausted or disenchanted lovers. We must remember, though, that the famous sheikh Nafzawi, who was very knowledgeable on the matter, opted for the raw against the cooked vegetable. And his book is called *The Fragrant Meadow*!

Of course, God did not reserve the benefits, real or assumed, of the onion only to the Muslims, or to the Arabs. But when He created this Holy Alliacea,[2] which is made up entirely of successive layers, He was certainly already thinking of what the Moroccans were going to do with it some time later. Dishes comparable to the *qammama tadgines* have not been invented anywhere else in the world, not even in India, another onion heaven. According to Zette Guinaudeau, the author of the best book on Moroccan Cuisine, anyone can cook them, as long as they don't have "their onions burnt," that they are not in a hurry, as we say in the Near East. There are three types of *qammama*: the first one is with

[2]Of the same family as the garlic

honey and caramelized onions; the second one is with a sweet onion puree, filled with raisins and browned in the oven; and the third one is also seasoned with ginger and saffron, but has lemon, and cumin instead of cinnamon. Lamb tastes wonderful with the three kinds of *tadgines*. So does chicken. I personally think that chicken tastes even better than lamb. As for beef, which is sometimes cooked as a *tadgine*, my advice is to eat it as a stew.

Thus, is it not absurd that not one Moroccan poet has ever sung the praises of the onion? For something which was far less tasty than a *qammama tadgine*, the Chilean poet Pablo Neruda wrote a magnificent ode to the onion: "I will also remind people of how much your influence enriches a salad, and how heaven, by giving you the delicate shape of a hailstone, celebrates your vividly broken brightness on the hemispheres of a tomato."

P for Pomegranate

For the Greeks, the pomegranate was Aphrodrite's attribute; a symbol for love and it was the same symbol in the *Song of Solomon*. The King, who was quite well versed on the matter, mentioned the pomegranate four times when talking about the Shulamite. The fruit does have a thick rind, a not too feminine and unfriendly armor, which looks like leather or copper. But the pomegranate's roundness and bright color, when it reveals itself, largely make up for its outward ugliness. In *Les Nourritures terrestres*, André Gide wrote about its fascinating architecture—"a kept treasure, and the partitions of a beehive." Moreover, the pomegranate flower, *jullanar*, is the brightest of all flowers, and its praises were sung by scores of Persian and Arab poets. According to Ferdowsi, *jullanar* it is a combination of fire and blood. No wonder it can only be compared to the burning cheeks of a loved one. And since one metaphor calls for another, of course it has been said, that the lips of a lover, "taste like pomegranate syrup," and "from her silver breast, grow two pomegranates." Even if these images, the last one especially, has become trite, but they were long popular among certain poets. In order to sing of his love for women, Ibn al-Rumi, a more sensual precursor of Arcimboldo,[3] evoked images of undulating branches, apples, pomegranates, and bunches of purple grapes.

Need I say that the pomegranate is not used in dessert baskets, as Alexandre Dumas seemed to think? Its sweet and sour, even acidic, juice was once as much sought after as *verjus* or lemon. Because of its garnet color, Ibn al-'Adim used it often and judiciously whenever he cooked chicken. Today's *dibs* is concentrated, and used in many salads, purees, stews, and panades, from the Near-East to as far as Iran. As for the very acidic fresh seeds, they mix very well with the toasted eggplants of *baba ghannouj* (literally "Dressed up Daddy") which never fails to deliver when dressed with them.

Q for *Qata'if*

❖

These thick pancakes are cooked on a metallic grill and sprinkled with honey, *raisiné*, or sugar syrup. They were already mentioned

---

[3]Guiseppe Arcimboldo (1527–1593), an Italian portraitist who painted faces made up of fruits and vegetables

in Ibn al-Rumi's *Diwan*, Hariri's *Seances*, or Mas'udi's *Golden Meadows*. As Ibn Mansur and Firuzabadi explained, they were given their name because they were as soft as velvet (*qatifa*) . . . The disciples of these lexicographers of the 14th century C.E. added that they could, like velvet, be either folded, or rolled up. But nobody has ever tried to explain why this word is almost never used in the singular form. Perhaps the word was borrowed, in the culinary field, from another language, and remained unchanged in its form, which is used infrequently. Or else *qata'ifs* were long ago filled with nuts or cream, and layered on top of each other, or maybe, as one big eater from Damascus once suggested, a normal man or woman would not be content with less than three *qata'ifs*!

It is very difficult to decide on this issue, since these pancakes are not all the same size or the same consistency, and they do not have the same trimmings. In Syria, for example, there are large, medium and small-sized *qata'ifs*, and each requires a particular treatment. The large ones, cousins to Moroccan *bghir*, are very different from Tetouan's *qata'if*. They are copiously spread with *samn*, sprinkled with sugar, and seasoned with a pinch of cinnamon. When you eat one, as is customary, during the month of Ramadan, at the end of *iftar*, you are then set to take on a new day of fast. The medium ones require more skill, and a larger stomach, since they are stuffed with walnuts, cheese, or cream before they are fried, and dipped into sugar syrup. Let us say right off the bat, one, or two at the most, can fill up one robust fellow. As for the small ones, they are just spread with some *crème fraiche*, and sprinkled with some sugar syrup. Anybody can eat a good dozen of them, at any time of the day or night. In Damascus, they bear the poetical name of *'asafiri* or "little birds," and in Alep the indecent nickname of *shlikkat mgharra'a*, or, literally, "swallowed down whores," which is a way of saying that in both cases they are very, very light.

R for *Ras al-hanut*

❖

The authors of the *Larousse Gastronomique*, who are usually quite knowledgeable, are greatly mistaken when they reduce *ras al-hanut* to a mixture of three spices, typically clove, cinnamon, and black pepper, with some dried rosebuds added to sweeten the powder. They are also wrong when they suggest using it with "stews," without saying which ones, or even using it with cous-cous broth. It looks as though our gourmets got their information from the label of a pretty jar of *ras al-hanut* at their local super-market, and that they took the manufacturer's advice seriously!

Those who do want to find out exactly what *ras al-hanut* is all about will once more have to take a look at Zette Guinaudeau's book. She gives the list of the twenty-seven spices that go into the mixture. As you read it, it looks as though Ibn Battuta himself gathered a good number of these spices as he traveled about in Asia and Africa, and brought them back to his native country. There is Malabar's cardamom, Sumatra's mace, China's galanga, Sudan's strong-smelling tara, Malaysia's long pepper, Borneo's cubebe, and many other products, sometimes from America—as well as belladonna (very little of it, of course), and the terrible cantharis,[4] allegedly an effective, aphrodisiac beetle.

As for the uses of *ras al-hanut,* they should not be limited to a few dishes. It is good with game, red squash and honey *tadgine,* and *mruziyya,* an authentic lamb preserve, which is ritually cooked on the day of the Sacrifice. You also need *ras al-hanut,*

[4] a.k.a. Spanish fly

hashish and honey, almonds and nuts, ginger and an extra dose of cantharis, to cook the famous *ma'jun*, which is both a narcotic and an aphrodisiac. You will lose your footing as you eat it, but this does not mean that you won't fly far, far away.

S for Sesame

Sesame is known in France because of Ali Baba. Actually, this pleasant character from *The Thousand and One Nights* has done nothing to promote the oily plant that we Arabs have always known, and loved! But, since the mid 19th century C.E., the magic formula, "Open, Sesame," which he uttered at the entrance of the cave of the forty robbers has become the archetypal name for a password in French. Police detective San Antonio[5] uses the word "sesame" in the sense of a "master key," and true enough, no door, and no woman, can resist his "sesame."

Our own sesame is no less efficient. We use its seeds in our bakeries, kitchens, and in desserts, from Morocco to Iraq. We make oil out of it, called *sirej (shayraj* in classical Arabic, from the Persian *shirah*). It is very useful, because it has a neutral taste, and can be used in cooking over high heat without a breakdown of its chemical properties. We also use it in our *tahini*, which is a staple in the Near East. Without *tahini*, there would be no *hummus*, no *tarator* to accompany our fish, no "eggplant caviar," as they say on this side of the Mediterranean, with a tad of exaggeration . . .

---

[5] Frederic Dard (1921–2000) wrote no less than 260 books with San Antonio! His books started like the typical thriller stories, but over the years, Dard developed his own language—a very rare thing, in France. San Antonio has been extremely popular for years.

And, here, I am purposely only mentioning the dishes which restaurant chefs and caterers have been successful serving in France! There are so many more dishes, which we eat in our homes. We use *tahini* with certain vegetables, like the squash, the beet, or certain meats or fish. Besides, those who love sweets, must know that sesame cream is indispensable in *halawa (halva)*, which is much more subtle than you might be lead to think by standardized cans.

Once sesame has been pressed or crushed, we are left with what our ancestors called *kush*, and we eat that too, when we do not have much money. We spread it on bread, with a few drops of *sirej*. This is what Ali Baba must have done before he robbed from the thieves . . .

S for Spinach

According to Ibn al-'Awwam, the famous Andalusian agronomist who lived in the 12th century C.E., spinach is *ra'is*, the king of vegetables. *Isfanakh*, or *isbanakh*, as it was then called, comes from Persia, and was unknown to both Greeks and Romans. It was introduced in Spain rather late, possibly in the middle of the 10th century C.E. The Eastern Arabs, who had brought spinach to Spain, did not, at that time, eat it very much either. There is no mention of spinach in classical Arabic scientific literature before Razes and Ibn Wahshiyya. Both lived in Iraq in the 10th century C.E. so how can we explain Ibn al-'Awwam's claim of the dominance of spinach over the garden and kitchen "aristocrats," like the eggplant and the asparagus? How can we explain its irresistible, wide acceptance?

The answer is spelled out in *Nabatean Agriculture*, by Ibn Wahshiyya, who said spinach is considered "the most innocent" of all vegetables. The fact that it became the *ra'is* in so short a time, without losing its innocence in the process, could be considered a very moralistic parable. A parable that shows how different human beings are from plants.

T for Tadgine

Europe has now become acquainted with this round, varnished earthenware dish with a pointed cover. The Moroccans cook in it, keep their dishes hot in it, and serve from it the most succulent stews ever imagined. Some of my French friends are starting to learn about a few of these stews, and it always makes me happy to hear them compare the merits of *mqalli, q'dra, mshermel* and *mderbel.*

But very few people know that the word *"tadgine"* (*tajin* or *tayjan* in classical Arabic) has a Greek origin. It is derived from *tagenon,* or *teganon,* which means "frying pan." It is mentioned as such in Medieval Arab literature, along with the words *miqla* and *miqlat.* Razin, the Andalusian gourmet of the 13th century C.E. mentioned cast iron as well as earthenware *tadgines,* and they could be varnished, but do not have to be. However, not one dish in his book was named after this piece of cooking equipment, nor can we find one mention of *"mutajjan,"* a word derived from *tajin,* which was used by another Arab gourmet, Warraq. Curiously, this Iraqi ignored the word *tajin* in his chapter on cooking equipment, but he mentioned eight recipes for *mutajjanat,* which were invented for Baghdad's caliphs, one of whom was the famous Harun al-Rashid. All of them were fowl dishes fried in oil. They were different, he said, from *tabahajat*, which were cooked in the same way, but with the meat of four-legged animals.

This said, we could assert that at the time Ibn Razin wrote his book, in about 1250 C.E., the word *tajin* already had different meanings. In a famous anonymous treatise on cuisine, which was written in Muslim Spain (or in Morocco) some thirty years earlier, the author designated some kind of earthenware for the oven, as well as a dish, which was thickened with a few eggs. Those were still a far cry from today's *tadgines*, but they were somewhat of a beginning . . .

U for *Utrujj*

By paying homage to *utrujj*, possibly the first citrus fruit ever known to the Arabs, I am only abiding by a *sunna* of our Prophet as confirmed by an authentic *hadith*: "The faithful who recite the Koran are comparable to the *utrujj*, whose taste is exquisite, and whose scent is intoxicating." I sometimes wonder if the Prophet was speaking of the citron (the *kabbad*), which I ate as a child, or of another of the large family of citrus fruits. In any case, it could not be the sweet orange (*narunj*), or the lemon (*laymun*), because they were not introduced in the Near East until the 9th century C.E. through Persia, and then Oman, according to the historian Mas'udi. Let us therefore decide in favor of the citron, which has become so rare these days. It is round and covered with bumps, its rind is very thick, and it gives out very little juice, but its taste is sweet, and its smell is very strong. The Jews are very fond of using it often and claim that it is the hadar mentioned in Leviticus. This means that it has been in Palestine and in the surrounding countries for a very long time.

According to Muslim writers, the *utrujj* is made up of four elements, which are all useful to man: its rind is a perfume, its flesh a fruit, its juice a condiment, and its seeds a medicine against snakebites. It has another secret virtue, which was once very highly esteemed, but has become quite useless these days: "To find out whether a woman is a virgin or not," the physician Dawud al-Antaki wrote in the late 16th century C.E., "make her sniff some citron powder. If she does not sneeze, she is no virgin!"

V for Vinegar

❖

"Come thou hither and eat of the bread, and dip thy morsel in the vinegar." According to the Old Testament, this is how Boaz, seeing Ruth gleaning in his fields, invited her to partake of the meal of the reapers. This meal was indeed too rustic, but we know, thanks to an authentic *hadith*, that some twelve centuries later, the wives of the Prophet one day served it to him. He enjoyed it, and called for God's blessing on the vinegar. This is probably why the Muslims have nothing against vinegar, though it is made from an illicit product. They put it in many sauces, such as in their *mukhallal, sikbaj, zirbaj,* and *bazmaward.*

I will not write much about *mukhallal*—pickled turnips, eggplants, or cucumbers, because everybody knows of them. But the other dishes, which are definitely Persian, deserve to be mentioned. *Sikbaj*, was supposedly the favorite of the Sassanid king Khosrow, long before caliph Harun al Rashid and his son Al-Amin were crazy about it. It is a stew with vegetables (onions, leeks, eggplant . . .) and a piece of fatty meat. The ingredients are first boiled in water, with cinnamon and cilantro, then in a mixture of vinegar (*sik* in Persian) and *raisiné*. Arab cuisines, unfortunately, have not kept the recipe, but there is memory of it, the Spanish marinade, *escabeche*, whose name evidently comes from *sikbaj*, though the *Larousse Gastronomique* disagrees.

There is no trace either of *zirbaj*. We know that they were hen or chicken stews, sometimes savory, sometimes sweet and sour. Prince Ibrahim al-Mahdi excelled in cooking them. He associated the vinegar with quince juice. The same thing with *bazmaward* stews. The most easily digestible of this "banquet dish," as written by Iraq's Baghdadi in the 13th century C.E., called for simply a lukewarm roast, fresh mint, salted lemon, and walnuts cut in two. These ingredients were to be pounded with vinegar and rose water, and the meat paste was then stuffed into a hollowed loaf of bread. The loaf was cut into a rectangle, then placed between two layers of fresh mint in an earthenware dish, and finally sprinkled with some rose water. The taste is totally different from what you generally eat, but this is far better than the usual tidbits attributed to the Earl of Sandwich . . .

Beside gastronomy, it is to be noted that in spite of its sour taste—and possibly because of it—vinegar has often contributed to sweetening the lives of our ancestors. In particular, I am thinking of their sex lives, even though I know of Razes's very negative judgment of vinegar as he thought that vinegar was a terrible aphrodisiac, at least for some people. But the priestesses of Venus would not have used it so much, well into the last century, had its antiseptic, contraceptive and abortive virtues not compensated for its cold humor! And I am not speaking about those young ladies who knew how to make use of its very special virtue on the eve of their wedding day: Vinegar helps to constrict certain membranes.

W for Warraq

All that we know about Abu Muhammad al-Muzaffar ibn Nasr ibn Sayyar al-Warraq is from what he chose to write about himself in his *Kitab al-Tabikh (Treatise on Food)*. From his name, we can learn that he had a bookstore. From his documentation, we also know that he lived in the second half of the 10th century C.E., and possibly in Baghdad. His style betrays some literary knowledge, but it is nothing spectacular. Warraq had the same culture as many other educated men of his time. He must have loved food very much. Actually, he must have been obsessed with good food, since he wrote a book consisting of one hundred thirty-two chapters on the subject!

His *Kitab al-Tabikh* is a master book indeed, not only because it is the oldest to report on Islam's culinary art, but also because its author, a modest copyist, often quoted his sources. What a relief, since the first Arab manuscripts on the subject were lost—in particular, the book of Prince Ibrahim al-Mahdi, the Precursor, 779–839 C.E.! Warraq attributed some of these manuscripts to caliphs Al-Ma'mun (d. 833 C.E.), Al-Wathiq (d. 847 C.E.), and Al-Mut'tamid (d. 892 C.E.). One of them was allegedly written by vizier Yahya al-Barmaki (d. 805 C.E.), and another by the Christian physician Ibn Masawayh (d. 857 C.E.). There were four other treatises attributed to totally unknown authors, one of whom was Abu Samin (Fat Daddy!). If you add those authors to Al-Nadim's bibliography, which was written at the end of the 10th century C.E., the list of all the Arabs who wrote about food is impressive. This says a lot about the appetite of my ancestors, when they were the actors, and not the spectators, of history.

Obviously an impatient reader does not read such a book. Its bizarre vocabulary turns off many a reader, but as soon as one gets used to it, one is able to realize to what extent each of these recipes was carefully studied, and to what extent each flavor, and each color, was specifically considered with a view to nourish the reader's body and mind. The book begins with a 30 chapter essay on the humeral nature of food; it also deals with kitchen equipment, diet, exercise, and what is proper to eat in winter and in summer. I read that the Persian kings imposed silence at their tables, contrary to Al-Hasan, the Prophet's grandson, who allegedly told his contemporaries: "Stay a long time at the table, and talk a lot, for these moments are added to our lives." May his memory be blessed forever!

W for Watermelon

❖

Whereas the Southern Europeans have known it for a long time, mass summertime travel has only recently acquainted their Northern brethren with the watermelon. They enjoy it as soon as they set foot in Tunisia, Morocco, Spain or Turkey, and as quickly as they take pleasure in the hot sandy beaches and the sun's rays. As if in a competition, they wonder who can eat the most. Beginning at breakfast, they eat watermelon three times a day, especially if it's included in their food-and-board hotel plan. As they watch this competition, the locals gently play with their mustaches and have a good laugh, because, of all the fruits that God has ever created, they personally prefer the blondes!

This chapter, about the relationship between the North and South, is the end of a long and winding history. Watermelon actually originated in Subtropical Africa. It was bitter and not much different from the gourd. From there, it was somehow sent to India, and no one knows why, or how. There it started to get sweeter. From India it launched its *taghriba* (Western journey) to Afghanistan first, then Iran, then Mesopotamia, and so on, and at every step, it was given the name of the country from which it originated: "Indian melon" in Iraq and Syria, "Palestinian melon" in Egypt, and "Algiers' melon" in Spain. Contrary to our general beliefs, the journey of the watermelon to the West occurred quite late, probably during the 9th century C.E. The watermelon was indeed mentioned here and there, from Baghdad to Cordoba, in the 10th century, but it was not before the 13th century C.E., even the 14th century, that it finally became a familiar fruit. Until then, the word *bittikh* (pronounced *battikh*), which became *batèque* in French, then *pastèque*, was used for "melon." It was so popular that the Arab fruit and vegetable marketplaces were called *dar al-bittikh*.

To tell the truth, because of numerous historical and geographical variations, which occurred over time, even the best linguists are apt to get confused while trying to discern the various names of the watermelon from those of the muskmelon. This is often the case with the turbulent tribe of the *Cucumis, cucurbits* and other *cucurbitaceas . . .*

X for . . .

❖

"X" could be a mysterious plant, an unknown recipe, or a secret medicine, but I have decided that it will be an anonymous writer.

A few years ago, he would probably have been the Andalusian writer who compiled the extraordinary book of recipes called *Kitab al-Tabikh fi al-Maghrib wa al-Andalus* in the late 12th century C.E., or maybe in the early 13th century C.E. In spite of its aberrant layout, perhaps due to the dispersion of the manuscript, this book gives us a remarkable account of the culinary art of the Muslim West, from Spain to Tunisia. It records the local components of *al-Andalus* cuisine—in particular the cuisine of the Berbers—but also reveals all the things which are owed to the East.

However, today it seems more urgent to me to celebrate the memory of another anonymous author. He was most likely an Egyptian. His *Kanz al-fawa'id* ("The Treasure of Tricks"), which was the object of a very comprehensive study, was published four years ago. Every page contains an unsuspected wealth of information, which makes it possible to complete, specify, and correct what was considered givens from other books previously written on the subject or from others written after. Considering its 830 recipes, every culinary historian will have a lot to work on for quite some time; the lexicographers will have a veritable treasure chest from which to enlarge their dictionaries; and the enlightened amateurs will be assured hours and hours of fascinating discoveries. I was amazed to find out that the Easterners already knew how to make many sauces at the time of the Mameluks. They were called *sals* (from the Latin *salsus*). Another sauce, *jajiq* (a yogurt preparation), did not wait for the Ottoman sultan Selim the first to conquer Egypt, and the Arabs were at that time making *Hallum* cheese. Today, they import it from Cyprus.

Y for Yogurt

❖

In spite of its name, *Lactobacillus bulgaricus*, and with due respect to the Bulgarians, I believe that this pleasant germ, which turns milk into yogurt, is more at ease in the Near East than in the Balkans. It does achieve a few miracles in other Eastern countries, like India, Iran or Turkey, but none of these countries, not even Turkey, produces a yogurt "cheese" that is comparable to *labne*, especially when it is rolled into small balls, and the balls are kept in olive oil. And whereas many countries can rightfully claim to be the inventors, under a great many different names, of *kishk* (*bulgur* wheat mixed with yogurt, dried in the sun, then crushed into a powder), or *dubeke* (a yogurt with the liquid drained out, then boiled, salted and kept in a jar for the winter), the Near-Eastern Arabs, those who live in cities and those who live in smaller towns, and the nomadic Bedouins, are the only ones who make a point of having yogurt every day, and almost at every meal.

This passion is expressed in different ways: from the most simple, a bowl of yogurt to be eaten with other dishes, to the authentic yogurt cuisine, in which yogurt is used, cold or hot, to accompany meat and vegetables. I consider *sheikh al-Mahshi* (zucchini, squash or eggplants stuffed with ground meat and pine nuts, cooked in yogurt), and *labaniyye* (*kebbe* balls stuffed with fat and nuts, cooked in the same manner) to be the two masterpieces of this cuisine. *Labaniyye* is at its very best when added to fresh fava beans and seasoned with tarragon. As for those cold Near-Eastern dishes with raw (cucumber), or cooked (eggplant, spinach, chard . . .) vegetables, I will not say much, because one can enjoy excellent dishes like these in other countries, including Bulgaria.

As a way of apologizing, I am happy to quote below a deliciously nonsensical syllogism, which a Bulgarian lady once taught me:

The Bulgarians eat a lot of yogurt.
The Bulgarians live a very long time.
So eat a lot of yogurt
If you want to become an old Bulgarian!

Z for Ziryab

As far as I know, there are two of them.

The first one—the authentic one—was an excellent musician, a subtle gourmet, and a refined human being, who for a long time looked for his Andalusia in Iraq, and eventually found it in Islam's Far West. He died in 857 C.E.

The second one—the author of these lines—has borrowed his name for six years now and still does not understand how he had the nerve to do that. His only excuse is that he loves to eat and drink, and perhaps even more, to talk about it. So, before closing this lexicon, he humbly begs your indulgence.

The name Ziryab—the "blackbird"—who left his native Iraq around the year 820 C.E. in order to settle in Cordoba, Spain, is synonymous with grace and elegance, as well as perpetual renewal. An extraordinary musician, he allegedly founded the Andalusian school of music. He is also believed to have invented the five-string lute. He was a poet. He knew the lyrics and tunes of ten thousand songs by heart. He was a geographer and an astronomer. A gourmet, he introduced the asparagus to Spain, he advocated for haute cuisine, and he reformed the art of table manners. He also created something like a beauty salon, where people could learn how to comb their hair, apply make-up, use perfume, and dress appropriately for each season . . .

By signing with the name of Ziryab his culinary chronicles, which were first printed in *Qantara* magazine, and now gathered into this book, the author has wished to pay homage to the black freedman who had become Cordoba's arbiter of taste, and another Petronius or Brummel. Arab gourmet traditions, from the Near East to Maghreb, are here presented for the first time together, through scholarly references, literature quotes, historical anecdotes, travel notes, and recipes. All of them concur in highlighting the cultural crossbreeding which Islam deliberately developed for at least ten centuries.

Farouk Mardam-Bey was born in Damascus, Syria, in 1944 C.E. He is in charge of the *Sindbad* collection at *Actes Sud*. He is the author, with Robert Bistolfi, of *The Treatise of the Chickpea* (*Sindbad-Actes Sud*, 1998), and writes gastronomic chronicles for *Qantara*, the quarterly journal of the *Institut du Monde Arabe*, in Paris, France.